TRANSFORMATION

TRANSFORMATION

LIFE BEFORE BIRTH,
COSMIC CONSCIOUSNESS
AND
ALTERNATE REALITIES

R.A. BLAYNEY

**AbSent
Publishing**

Transformation: Life Before Birth, Cosmic Consciousness and Alternate Realities.

Absent Publishing.

Cover image by Johan Swanepoel/Shutterstock.

The author can be contacted at, www.rablayney.com.

Library of Congress catalog number available upon request.

ISBN 978-0-9865707-1-1
Ebook ISBN 978-0-9865707-2-8

Contents

Introduction

Anyone who has ever wondered about life and whether we exist after death is about to take a journey into some of the most intuitive stirrings of our mind. More than that, the question of whether we exist before even being born will come into sharper focus. It is something many of us have known but have eventually forgotten through the course of our lives. The lingering knowledge of what we are is the force that pushes us to the brink of what we believe to be real and otherwise imagined.

What we describe as death is a very similar experience to being born into life. If we were to be born and then die the same day, the experience would be as if we were waking from a dream and then falling back into it again. This notion may sound bizarre, but while some who read these words will think the concept preposterous, there will be others out there who will know exactly of what I speak.

The following is based on my experience of being completely lucid while moving into the world we call physical reality. But it goes much further than mere definitions of life and death. Beyond those ideas is a world of realities that transcends concepts of space and time and what it means to exist. It offers an explanation on how we continue beyond this reality into higher realms of awareness. The larger picture is how we come to be in those alternate realities and how those realities could possibly exist. Yet, there is very much an explanation—scientific, as well as spiritual—for *how* they exist. Through these pages we will come to know a great deal about alternate existence in ways many of us may have never considered, some of which will at times seem beyond belief.

Anyone who has died even just briefly, or has lost a loved one, or who recoils constantly at the thought of their own death, will hopefully find some answers through the experiences I am about to recount. If we hope to discover something more about ourselves, this one step could unleash a plethora of possibilities that may have always been close to the reader's heart.

It is actually before we are even conceived that existence remains far removed from what we come to understand as our life. In order to realize existence beyond the physical definition we have devised as our mainstay, we must look at reality in a completely different way than to what we have become accustomed. That which we accept as real and what we believe to be our life defines our existence at any given moment.

Those who have had a Near Death Experience will emphatically swear there is an afterlife. I have never gone through such an event, or at least not in the way most are recalled. My own experience is quite different from those popular descriptions we read in magazines, hear on talk shows, share by way of social media and discover through books. Yet, by the time the reader has finished these chapters to the very conclusion there should remain a lingering thought. What I have experienced is something many people do not usually speak of, but at the same time it is something as old as our existence. Those who remember waking into physical life generally find the experience so strange and overwhelming it is often given up as a brief whimsy that must have been nothing more than a perplexing hallucination. The experience is so departed from what we come to know as our existence here in the world that it is often abandoned and forgotten for our mere inability to describe what later seems so unreal.

When I began writing this I did not realize it at the time, but my research would open up doors and force me to see that for as long as human beings have existed we have simultaneously walked alongside another reality. This reality is as much about death as it is about life. What is most unique about the things I am going to share is that if this strange transformation has happened to me it has certainly happened to others, if not actually every living person who has come into this world.

Furthermore, what I am about to describe does not require a belief in any particular religion. For anyone who is devoutly religious, this experience encompasses all religions while, at the same time, encompassing none of them at all. Everything we are and what we have come to believe ourselves to be is largely an illusion we have constructed for the sake of convenience. Our true existence is something that has been known by some of the oldest cultures that have lived throughout our history. In fact, while many of our own peoples have sprung to life and have reached pinnacles of mesmerizing achievement in a relatively short period, a number of these ancient cultures have lived alongside us through many thousands of years, quietly waiting for our next moment of enlightenment to be realized.

Through this book, we will examine what death and life may truly be. We will look at what we believe to be existence and how that belief may be wrong, or at least partly skewed. There will be points that may seem very strange and difficult to accept. All that is required by the reader in order to enjoy the content, however, is an open mind.

How and why we come to exist in this world is the strange and mysterious puzzle that keeps many of us questioning our own sense of being. Like any puzzle, we rarely gain a true glimpse of it—true insight—until we step far back and see it from a detached perspective. Until we do so, we are too close—too involved in everything—to understand what is happening to us and where we are heading as we wind our way through a bumpy existence. In the end, we all discover that none of it was ever really a mystery in the first place. Instead, it was a hazy fog, which gave us the opportunity to walk past it and see ourselves again as we were always meant.

Whether we believe in an afterlife, 'before life', or whether we cling to religious convictions, all of us throughout time have held onto a sense—a belief—in something far beyond our physical interpretation of reality. Since human beings have existed, all of us have been certain there is something more, hidden behind a curtain we spend most of our lives unable to see, but continue to feel.

As we get deeper into the subject matter, I will explore alternative perspectives on reality that some readers may have never imagined. There are ever evolving thoughts and perceptions of our existence and our place in the universe that are currently turning modern physics inside out. Yet, despite a certain bizarre aspect owing to this element, many leading physicists are seriously considering that our existence may be much more strange and difficult to quantify than we ever imagined.

But I am getting a bit ahead of myself.

I have divided the content of this text into three parts. The first part is about my experience of coming into this existence, along with the memories I carried that are responsible for my perceiving the world as I do. Through this, along with the many other events in which I have been involved since then, I have come to realize physical existence as something apart from what we really are. During the first four chapters, I touch upon certain events I have had throughout my life and offer what I have come to learn from them, along with research I have conducted as an explanation for our mystical journey.

In the second part of the book, I have presented some aspects and postulations as to why our reality and existence is the way we interpret it and why we sense there is something beyond our immediate point of view. Throughout various transparencies I have noted between life and death, I have also seen parallels in modern physics. The second part is largely my attempt to rationalize those physical studies with certain spiritual philosophies.

Finally, part three offers up my overall interpretation of why we continue to exist and keep coming back into the physical world. At the same time we consider how ancient philosophies have defined this habit of ours and why we continue to partake in it.

It is the content of all three parts that combine with one another in order to properly describe this expanded awareness.

We are about to take a trip that should leave the reader thinking about existence in an ever broadening scope. At the very least, I hope the words written here are inspiring, thought provoking and that they offer some answers to the question of who we are and why we are here. More importantly, I hope everyone who reads these words and has ever doubted the purpose of their existence realizes there is something far more than what we merely see around us.

1

Awakening

*Everything is illusion, until it engulfs us
so completely it becomes real.*

I awoke from a dream, only to find I was inside another dream. This is how I remember being born.

It may sound strange, but there are a number of people who remember this one, singular moment. Some are even able to recall more than just that. While there are those who actually retain their lucidity when moving into a physical reality, it is odd that in our corner of the world many of us lose those memories along the way. For a great many more who live in far off regions of the globe, such experiences are actually more common than many of us here in the West are aware.

When we move from pure conscious awareness into a

physical life, the experience is a perplexing thing for anyone who remembers the event. It is disorienting while at the same time reaffirming. The transformation of existence from one form into another is something that has no similarities for most of us through everyday life, except one. Being born into the reality we come to know is quite similar to waking from a dream. It is also reminiscent of falling into a dream, from which we can not escape.

This is the closest thing to the experience of becoming born which is comparable to something we can understand while we are alive in this world. The irony is that even with that, a great many of us still do not know what to make of the separation between waking and dreaming reality. This is why it is so difficult to explain what lucid awareness is like when we pass from an ethereal existence into one that is physical. Nevertheless, what follows is my best attempt to describe the experience of such a mystical event.

My first awareness of physically existing came over me gradually. It pushed me from what I knew before to what was now altering my perception toward something that was still forming. I began moving from a tepid awareness into a reality I was not yet ready to embrace. The harshness of the moment became increasingly sharp. At the same time a fog began filling me up, dimming the sense of what I had always been up to that moment, the clarity becoming obscured the more this new life took shape.

It soon became clear I was changing. That sensation began turning to a form of irritation as the world took hold of my growing sense and I began to feel the tight grip of physical reality.

Awakening

There was nothing glorious or illuminating about being born. I briefly struggled against it. By the time I realized I was in the world, there was nothing else to be done. I became lost in the instant as it swept me away.

It can not be understated that being born into a physical life is a truly awkward affair. I am not sure why, but it was upon birth that my perception began to alter markedly. Moving from one reality into another is an experience that is both strange and somehow evocative. It is as if we have fallen asleep and woken up at the same time.

While the experience of how I came to physically exist was appropriately mystifying, I do not think it is unique to how many of us come into this world. The only difference between my experience and that of some others is even though I was completely aware during my transformation from a separate existence into this one, I was able to maintain the memory throughout my life. How many of us come to forget those memories seems to be the result of our physical life consuming us, along with what we are soon taught to believe as we grow into easily impressionable young people.

I have little doubt every one of us comes into this world teetering on a precipice of what was real before and what is real at the moment of our awakening into corporeal reality.

To be more precise, I did not so much awake from one dream into another. It was my existence before then which briefly remained the reality while my birth appeared as the mirage. Only after some time went by did the mirage of this new life become the reality, while that place from where I had come gradually took on the qualities of a dream.

Physical existence, as it first begins to form, is not

immediately persuasive. It somehow feels wrong and unnatural, even though we gradually come to accept it as a reality which is being forced upon us. We quite likely all go through a similar realization, though the meaning is eventually lost to many. Anyone who remembers their birth and what it was like to have their cognition changed will surely find it difficult to put into words. I can only say that immediately before I came into this life I was not aware of drifting about in the womb, or growing, or of hearing voices outside that idiosyncratic environment. It seemed my consciousness was somewhere other than the world I would eventually come to know.

Some years went by before I would clearly see that existence—all of it—whether awake, asleep, alive or even dead, is nothing more than variations of our conscious perception of what we interpret as real. This form of being is a matter of perspective as we continue to exist from one reality to another. Moving through different states of existence involves a transformation of our consciousness to a level that all realities, in whatever form they may take, are equally valid. One is just as real as the next. It is that transformation of our awareness that often blinds us to the fact we are moving through various states of reality without even knowing it.

This is why being born is so similar to becoming aware of a lucid dream. We know it is not real, but it is real enough that we come to accept it. What is particularly peculiar is how we come to accept an existence which is largely illusion.

This is how bizarre and prone to perception our idea and acceptance of reality seems to be. In much the same way we fall into sleep, waking into physical life is very much like finding oneself inside a dream state, while sometimes not even aware of where we are, let alone *who* we are. And as we shall see, physical life turns out to be just one version of existence, which diverts us from a resounding truth that sometimes screams at us in silence.

From Ether to Substance

Migrating from one reality into another would be one of the most—if not *the* most—astounding events of my life. For many of us it is not even a memory, let alone a haunting nightmare that kicks us repeatedly as it urges us to wake from our slumber. By the time we are cognizant enough to make sense of this new world, everything before then is largely forgotten.

Physical existence allows us the luxury of drifting ignorantly from a truth that was more significant than many of us will remember. Soon after birth, the pain and conflicting sensation of physical reality takes over whatever we may have been aware of before then. Quickly enough, we find ourselves grappling with this new reality as we try to make sense of it.

Transformation is a segue from one form of consciousness into another. Of course, it would take some time for me to understand this. For much of the initial part of my new life, I remained at the mercy of the currents and tides of the world which now claimed me.

As I was taken from my entrance into this world and delivered to a hospital crib, I remember having to briefly swallow some saliva that was building inside my mouth. I thought how terribly uncomfortable that fairly insignificant act made me feel. Yet, at the very same time I was completely aware it was something I would have to get used to. It seemed to solidify the fact that this new existence was now real, casting away all previous doubt. I also knew if I wished to remember I had already existed before then, I would have to hang onto the memory of what was happening to me as tightly as I could. I knew beyond any doubt that if I did not it would all be soon forgotten.

While I was quite lucid of my transformation into life, it went much further than that. I had a profound knowledge of more than simply existing in this particular reality. It appeared I knew exactly what was taking place and what this world seemed to expect of me. I may have been initially disjointed, but I had an overwhelming sense of having gone through the very same thing before. As alien as it was, all the things that seemed strange were also strangely familiar.

I can only describe it now as traveling to a distant land which is unfamiliar at first glance. Once we recognize something about that land, we then remember having been there before and everything makes sense. As fragmented as it may have been, I also knew it would be another journey, though that realization would take some time to settle cohesively within my mind.

Awareness seems to alter constantly while this life remains a fading moment as we move past a world in which none of us were ever really meant to be.

After spending just several days in the hospital, my mother was soon sent home. Even now, I distinctly remember that time as if it had just happened.

Later, when I was older—a young adult in my twenties —I would describe to her what I experienced during those first few days of my existence. I particularly remember when she brought me home to her parents' house, several days following my grand entrance at the hospital. One of the first things she did was to feed me a bottle while sitting in the top floor bathroom of my grandparents' home. I remember gazing up at a tank high above us as a chain dangled from it within arm's reach. This was apparently how old fashioned toilets were once made. Years afterward, I would return to that house and see the toilet just as I remembered it.

To this day my mother does not know what to make of those memories. She admits that everything I described, in detail, was completely accurate. Being an educated woman, she insisted it should not be possible for me to retain any memories as a newborn, let alone have such a cognitive awareness of everything that was happening around me at such an infantile age. The human brain simply is not developed enough after barely a week of growth, she insisted. Yet, she could not deny the fact that I remembered everything so clearly.

Contrary to antiquated notions, there are presently a number of neuroscientists who have come to believe such things as consciousness and thought are a completely separate phenomenon, both of which operate independently of the physical brain.

David Chalmers, a renown philosopher and Professor of Neural Science at New York University, has done much work to explore these views. 'The Hard Problem', as he called it, was something he lectured on and examined at length while trying to define such existential questions as conscious thought as opposed to biological brain function. It is not surprising that doctors and researchers continue to struggle with such a dilemma when trying to separate or compose such topics of the mind. Scientists still are not sure how even such manifestations as visual perception are cognitively interpreted. If they are merely processes of the brain, one would think the subject would have been easier to dissect by now.

Fractured Existence

Not only did I come into the world knowing this life was not the beginning of my existence, I also seemed to know I would exist far beyond it. I had an undeniable sense I would only have to dwell within this new place for a short time. Like any hallucination, this one seemed fleeting.

Divined from my own encounter, that place beyond life did not appear as some beautiful or flowery mural. There were no heavenly visions that took my breath away as I moved from a Shangri-La to a world of pitter-patter, only to await a rebirth in paradise. It is more like an aching awareness that taps the back of one's head with a nagging persistence, until many of us become convinced we should merely forget it altogether; that it actually *was* nothing more than a hallucination.

As much as some would like to deny our existence as anything more than coincidence, it appears the reality is much more complex than that. From the moment we are born, our lives are nothing less than an awakening that is simply waiting for another chance to sleep.

Our awareness of it may be splintered, but we do move through variations of consciousness, even though we may not understand what is happening. Within our physical existence we go through a similar process every time we fall asleep. It is as if we are moving back into a lost memory of a world we once knew, only to have forgotten. Every morning we wake from our slumber, it is as if we have been born all over again. We are here in this world, but at the same time we are not. For as long as we live, we are only temporary shadows of ourselves. Each of us subconsciously glances back to what we were as our mind plays cat-and-mouse with the remnants of our creeping memories. It is only after years of making love to this life that we become convinced our present existence is truly real.

Our basic nature remains one of contradicting intrigue. For many, existence remains a riddle. The perplexity of physical life and from where we originate becomes something we eventually choose to forget. It is only on the day we gain clarity that we are on our way beyond this brief interlude in search of what we momentarily forgot. In a very real sense, we are nothing less than travelers in search of a lost path, knowing it will one day take us back from where we came.

In this sense, it is unfortunate we teach ourselves to fear death as some foreboding menace. In fact, the very opposite is true. Death is no more fearsome than the physical life we live, to the very moment we finally die. Our true meaning is often obscured as we become entangled in the physical whims and indulgences that is existence in this world. It is during our brief diversion of life that many of us lose touch with ourselves while living an existence that is far departed from our natural condition. Death is the one eventuality that reveals the truth of what we are and gives us the chance to see reality clearly once more.

At first, life is somehow displaced and out of sync with what we feel. The idea that we will continue to exist here in this place we later call the 'real' world initially seems hard to grasp. We begin to move in a single direction. Through a long drawn out process, we begin to believe— *truly* believe—this is the real world and nothing else exists beyond what we see around us. Lingering insights and dim memories are soon cast off.

It is said each one of us enters this life hearing a sound we eventually learn to ignore. That sound is our beating heart. It is as if we do not want any reminder that as long as we are alive and that sound continues, there will one day be the possibility the sound will finally stop. Our heartbeat is nothing less than a testament to how finite is our physical reality and that our time here is limited.

As we grow, we feel we will always inhabit this new land. It seems only through living and perpetual education, pounded mercilessly into our brain, that we later decide life is more fleeting than we would like. Some will choose to believe in a higher existence and a greater power while others will take comfort in their assertion they will simply no longer exist and will soon enough dissolve into earth. All the things we did—all our achievements and misdeeds —will eventually be lost.

Some of us will reach a point in our lives where we think of death and come to accept it as inescapable. Many of us will not want to make peace with the inevitable, but all the evidence will lead to that unavoidable conclusion—

we are all doomed from the moment we are born.

There will be those who tire themselves emotionally in an effort to plan for that undeniable end, even while many of them remain convinced they will never truly die. It is usually only after a close brush with death that some will move in that direction of planning and reconciling the reality.

The truth is that many of us will never be ready. When the time comes and we are one of those few who has the fortune to see we are slipping into the inevitable, a realization will come over us. Once we begin to fall into the eternal ether, we will understand that no prior planning will seem important any longer. As the world begins to fade away, none of those things will matter at all.

It is said some people, as they die, will likely think of their loved ones, or all the things that mattered to them most in this world. I can not speak to such aspects personally, but I can admit what I have experienced during those moments.

In all my cases of near death I have felt a profound separation from the world I have come to know.

During the last time I almost died—technically I did die, just briefly—all the things I had been through, along with all those things I was about to leave behind, meant nothing. I knew I was going back to that place from where I came. Any planning I had done, or failed to do, leading up to that moment simply did not matter anymore.

Contrary to what one might think, the experience did not give me some new, profound outlook on life once I was brought back to the land of the living. It remained just another reminder in a long line of reminders that the lives we lead here, while at times fun and sometimes horrific, are nothing more than a flicker in a dream we are either waking from, or into which we are falling deeper.

Closer to Death

The first time I almost died was due to drowning. What more fitting an end than to go out with a pain similar to that with which I had come in?

I was about four years of age at the time and had not yet learned to swim. My mother, along with her brother and sister, had traveled to the East coast to spend the day on the beach. Being quite young, I found the sea to be mesmerizing. Sunlight sparkled off each shallow wave like shimmering diamonds that danced across an infinite plane. The experience felt magical. It was the first time I had ever seen the ocean and like any naïve child I felt drawn by its hypnotic spell.

As I walked into the sea, cool waves licked at my waist and tempted me out more as I became increasingly curious at how far I could go. It was fun to see how high I could get the water up to my face, never even realizing the current was subtly pulling me further away. It was relaxing and exciting, all at same time.

I soon found myself peeled from the firm base below as I discovered, quite terrified, I could no longer touch the bottom with my feet. I splashed frantically, realizing I could not even get back to shore. Thrashing and pummeling the water around me, I eventually began to sink. The world closed off. There was nothing but silence and the murky deluge of the water as it quickly enveloped and pulled me under. I held my breath for as long as I could.

Then, as if someone had thrown me a life preserver, I felt the bottom of the seabed. I allowed myself to sink into it, until falling into a sitting position, grateful at having finally found a firm base. I bent my knees and pushed off against it with all my strength. Once I broke the surface of the water I began to holler and call out for help. While I did, I splashed about desperately, trying to claw my way back toward land.

Whatever momentum I had managed to gather in that moment soon faded and I began to sink to the bottom once more. Again, the silence and inevitability of utter helplessness swept over me. While I sank, I felt the water pulling at me more, dragging me deeper.

Like before, I eventually felt the ocean floor and pushed against it as hard as I could. It was a reprieve, but one I had already realized was fleeting. Although taking a little longer this time, I eventually broke the surface and, in a frenzy, began crying out as loudly as I could. Each time I did, water splashed into my mouth, partially choking me as I tried to call out. At the same time, I tried drastically to stay above water as I thrashed about. In that instant I realized anything on the surface was a chance at life while everything below was certain death. As panicked and frightened as I was, the acceptance of what was soon going to happen was already tightening around me.

Eventually, I ran out of strength and began sinking once more.

I felt an overwhelming sense I would not be coming up a third time. The world began to drift away and I was suddenly overcome by an odd sensation. I realized I was going to die—quite agonizingly, at that—but a peace took hold of me. As I sank to the bottom, I realized I would soon be going home. And that is the most clear and concise way I can think to describe it. My dread dissolved, along with any hope of life, as I realized there was absolutely nothing to fear in dying. Just as I had continued to feel my existence before being born, this experience seemed to be an echo of something calling back to me.

Then, the damnedest thing happened. As I was settling into returning to the world of my 'before life', something rudely yanked me from those very waters.

A man who had been sitting on the beach had apparently seen me in the process of drowning from the very start. My mother and her siblings were completely oblivious, but this one person happened to glimpse what was taking place while sitting complacently in the sand. He had dived into the water the moment he saw it begin to unfold. So, while I was in the process of drowning, thinking I was headed back to that overwhelming light we sometimes call everlasting consciousness, I was already in the process of being saved.

There was apparently some frenzied activity as I was unceremoniously dumped on the beach, by then barely conscious. Everyone gathered around, panic stricken as I was revived, coughing and choking up the water I had ingested. My unheralded savior then admonished my mother for not keeping a closer eye on me and stomped off in a huff, never to be heard from again.

Shortly after that, I was immersed in a rigorous swimming regimen at the local YMCA.

This was the first experience I had which succeeded in reminding me that life in this world is most certainly temporary and that we are all heading back to a place that remains part of us, no matter where we go.

As time went on I had a number of successive near death experiences (NDEs). As a child, several years following the drowning incident, I accidentally cut an artery in my wrist and proceeded to rapidly bleed out. Some quick work by the doctors, along with a blood transfusion, brought me back to the land of the living. To this day I still bear a scar on my wrist that looks as though I tried to commit suicide.

A number of other NDEs, as they are popularly termed these days, occurred over the following years. It seemed the universe either wanted me dead, or it was trying to humble me by impressing upon my senses just how temporary life is.

I was once hit by a spinning airplane propeller during an incident while working at a city airport. The large piece of whirling metal split my scalp open, but, for some reason, did not kill me. The employees and managers at the airport said it was the most remarkable thing they had ever seen. They recounted how the exact thing had happened to an employee years before—one of my predecessors—and how the spinning propeller had cleanly chopped his head in half. No one could understand how my head was still together following the incident, let alone how I could even be alive.

Once, I was also shot by a stray bullet while hunting. I actually saw the bullet coming directly toward me, but could not seem to move out of the way quickly enough to avoid it. The bullet hit me in the head but, miraculously, glanced off. By this time it seemed I had been blessed with a remarkably thick skull, something classmates and friends would later take delight in telling me, but not as a compliment.

TRANSFORMATION

Another annoying development I have experienced, just over the past several years, is a result of wasp stings. Though I have been stung by wasps countless times throughout my life with no adverse effect, other than some swelling, I eventually became allergic to the venom. The first occasion resulted in my going into anaphylactic shock, causing me to die briefly. Successive instances have brought me close to dying several other times.

Though I have been technically dead, at least twice so far, I did not experience a life altering vision. Perhaps I was not dead long enough for a brief trip to the afterlife. It could be that such visions are nothing less than a psychological phenomenon. Maybe it is a subconscious reaction that helps some people stay grounded in this life before their time to die has truly come. Or it could be that our consciousness briefly becomes detached from this world in such a fleeting manner that it becomes hallucinogenic and, at the same time, overwhelming.

Whatever it may be, my own experiences have continued to reinforce my sense of our altered realities and how we perceive our existence. I have absolutely no doubt we continue to live even after we die, though that may be something many of us still do not comprehend for as long as we are bound to our physical bodies. I am not so certain I share the same warm and rosy sense we all become connected with our loved ones after we die, as a number of people have professed. I feel it is more accurate to say we are all souls on a journey and that each one of us has our own path to follow, even in death. I have never had a sense that I came into this life while leaving loved ones behind from some prior existence. My own view is quite contrary to that 'feel good' imagery. I sense we travel our existence, in and out of one reality and another, all very much on our own. Even as much as I love my family here in the present, I do not have an overwhelming sense I will be united with them at the moment of my death.

Perhaps we meet past souls we have known during our life, or previous lives, but I do not believe or get the sense we spend the rest of eternity with them. I am more convinced we go on to find our own level of awareness. It is something for each of us to discover through mental growth and spiritual awakening. Maybe if we do have a near death experience, it is there to help some of us transition back through the existence we have in order to embrace the next one yet to be realized.

Seeing how fleeting life is and coming to accept that simple truth can be a great liberator. Once we are free to accept we are here only briefly and that dying is not such a bad thing, life takes on new meaning. We no longer have to worry about our hangups—all those things we hoped to accomplish, or all those things at which we failed. By finding some glimmer of happiness, no matter how simple a form that might take, and to find the resolve to be good to one another, we can be content that something worthwhile came from this life. It is finding just that one thing that makes the difference in the time we are here. That one thing might be to simply love someone, or to be loved, or to do nothing more than make a difference in some other person's life. The difference might be enough to alter that one person and make their own life better, no matter how meager the affect may be. Still, it could be sufficient that it changes their spirit and their outlook forever.

That is the truth of death. Once we realize it always walks with us and is a familiar companion that offers us respite, selfishness soon dissipates and we see the world around us in a clear light. The true importance of our brief existence then materializes to the point that all efforts put forth are far beyond our brief indulgence. Realizing we are all doomed to the same fate should unite us in its common affect, rather than drive us apart through familiar fear.

Perpetual Awareness

When we are born into this world, it may be accurate to suggest we all have some retained memories of the existence we had before coming here. Many of us wrestle with these lingering glimmers as children—those things that eventually come out of our subconscious knowledge in an effort to rationalize this existence with the one we just left behind. As time goes on, we convince ourselves all those subconscious stirrings are nothing but wavering delusions of childhood blunderings. We move on and grow up, forgetting silly notions and accepting our world as nothing more than what we see around us. Remembered or not, those lost insights remain as part of our being.

Humans are great creatures of adaptation. This is one of our more profound attributes. While it promotes our own survival, it is also the reason we come to accept the physical world around us and to carry out our ordained roles with so little question.

Looking back at my own experience, the world around me seemed ludicrous as a child. I had only begun to interact with it, but I already felt there was something very much out of place with how we exist physically. Perhaps this is because we sense deep down that the world is a distortion of what we know to be real.

It is explained in, *The Tibetan Book of the Dead*, that the physical world is not a natural existence for any of us. In my mind, even time seemed to be something that simply did not exist as I moved from one reality to the next. Time, I later discovered, is a perception that helps us quantify our existence. It seems we are fixated on always having a beginning and an end. The concept that time might simply always have been and always will be makes absolutely no sense to many of us. That the universe has always existed and always will exist is a frightening concept for some people. A number of us are simply incapable of mentally grasping the possibility.

In fitting fashion, our most accepted theory for the existence of the universe is the Big Bang. When I was young and enthralled with science it seemed to make perfect sense when explained in detail. After a while, however, I developed a problem with the whole theory. I kept wondering, what was there before the Big Bang. How could something not exist and then one day it suddenly *did* exist? It eventually began to seem like nothing more than a convenient answer to an impossible question.

Pundits point toward the universe's lingering electromagnetic radiation, otherwise known as Cosmic Microwave Background (CMB) radiation, citing it as a product of the Big Bang. It is the static that appears on a television when it is not tuned into a channel. However, no one can say definitively that it is truly the result of a massive explosion that brought the universe into being. The theory remains just that, but it is the best one with which scientists have been able to come up.

In spite of this overall concept, something about time

simply did not make sense even while I was still quite young. Everyone else who was already here before me seemed so obsessed with it. There was simply no sense of beginning and end as I moved into physical reality. This could explain the reason I was so sure my stay in this world would pass relatively fast.

The notion of infinity may seem esoteric. We naturally ask ourselves how anything could have no beginning and end. Yet, evidence of infinity exists all around us. Most of us simply choose to dismiss it for the simple reason it defies how we have been taught to perceive reality.

A simple example can be mathematically proved by taking two points and advancing one point toward the other, but always by only half the distance between them. If we imagine a ball moving toward a wall by only half the distance before it must come to a stop and then repeating the exercise, again advancing the ball by half the remaining distance, the math proves that each advance will carry on forever. The ball will continue to move toward the wall by half the remaining distance each time, but will never actually reach the end. The math will continue on forever. Math is the language of our physical nature, after all.

The exercise is reminiscent of solving the equation for *pi*. Theoretically, the decimal points for *pi* go on without end.

Even if we conducted this thought experiment with an actual ball, the movements would continue endlessly, but beyond the point of being practically measured. The ball would always move, but the movements would eventually become so minute that it would appear to be frozen in space while forever moving closer to the wall (we are measuring from the ball's closest surface to the wall, by the way).

Though the above exercise appears simple, there will be some who will never come to accept that this demonstration of infinite motion, while seemingly being frozen in space, could actually be real. It is a concept for our infinite reality and one we can not easily rationalize in a physical world that insists on a predetermined beginning and a set end.

That this exercise will force us to think beyond what we see and accept as real is the first hurdle in understanding that our finite perception and our infinite reality exist alongside each other. Both are actually varying aspects of what we consider to be real at any given moment. Existence, as we understand it, is something far beyond what we can actually define through convenient platitudes. Infinite existence is beyond our expectation, which is why we rarely grapple for anything more than what we can see and touch, or otherwise measure.

The truth is that if we simply dismissed any notion of time and distance, there would be no beginning to anything. There would also be no end. For as long as we exist in this world, those notions bind us here. The moment we realize there is no start and no stop, the world as we know it unfurls. Without those restrictive ideas, everything else makes sense. Existence and reality are as permeable as they have ever been, even while camouflaged and hidden from sight. Destroy the finite and eventually reality and existence come into clear focus. Only then do we see that infinity *is* existence.

Every one of us wakes up to our life with a boundless awareness. At the same time, we bring lingering remnants of our prior existence. As children, we believe we will live forever; that we are indestructible. It is understandable, given at that age we are still somewhat connected to the memory of having come into the world from another existence we sense is perpetual. While we are brand new people we have not fully learned the limitations of life and the expectations some of us later carry throughout our stay here.

Once our physical reality has firmly taken hold of us, however, the way we look at things begins to change. Life is no longer as endless as we had believed following our entrance into this world. Those who have been here for some time already, coupled with the restrictions we see on the surface, persuade us to eventually question our own existence. It is the wake-up call that either divides us or conforms us.

We are all heading for a more divine existence; possibly the place from where we came before there was time and space. Our essence was thrust into this reality, leaving us with many lifetimes to endure before getting back to where we belong. Perhaps this trap of repetitive existence is the reason why physical life becomes so convoluted and why some of us simply give up and allow ourselves to be absorbed into the mindset of the world in which we live.

Still, many of us doubt our present existence, which is another reason I believe we all carry a latent sense of what we were.

Perhaps as a way to deny the doldrums of our life, many of us believe we are put on this earth for a reason, and that we are meant to do something important that will change the world. That idea could be nothing more than an egocentric illusion. Such delusions may exist in our psyche for the mere sake that our lives mean something more significant than what we can glimpse in a fleeting moment of clouded hope.

It seems difficult to believe one person could change the nature of a whole race of human beings. History hints at certain individuals being placed among us in order to help us find our way. The final truth is there are few who are secure in placing our fate in the hands of a single oracle, whether they be the Buddha, Dalai Lama, Mahatma Ghandi or Jesus Christ. All these symbols of our own humanity are sent as reminders to help us stay on course, or bring us back in line. In the end, however, it remains that human nature always repeats itself.

I was lucky to have a mother who was a great follower of history, as well as various religions and philosophies. It was through her that I learned of such things as the Egyptian *Book of the Dead* and the *I Ching*. My own curiosity later drove me to explore Eastern philosophies through such texts as *The Tibetan Book of the Dead* and the *Tao Te Ching*. At the same time I continued to study concepts of science in astrophysics and quantum theory.

Over the years, I have noticed certain parallels can be drawn between modern physics and ancient, Eastern philosophies. Likewise, similarities can also be made between such religions as Christianity, Hinduism, Buddhism, Islam and a number of others.

Every religion centers around some belief in a Supreme Being and our lingering soul transcending after death. Either that, or the soul is recycled through another iteration of life experiences.

Many religions appear to be telling us the same thing

that quantum physics has lately shown to be true, but simply in another way that inevitably leads to a similar destination. It is up to each of us to find our own means to that same end.

In Chapter 5 and 8, I discuss different states of reality and touch on some quantum theory in order to help explain how these ideas converge with ancient philosophies. All contribute in order to validate the belief that the soul is a conscious awareness that carries on forever. Even Chapter 2 describes another state of existence wherein dreaming actually manifests a separate reality from the one in which we currently find ourselves. Chapter 3 goes on to reveal how we may all be consciously connected to one another, along with some scientific theories that help support this thought. Then, in Chapter 6, I discuss ancient beliefs and cultures, as well as lost civilizations. Chapter 7 goes so far as to explain how such phenomenon as UFOs and other strange topics may be a manifestation of just more separate realities.

As we shall soon see, much of the weirdness of physical existence has found some very real validation in science. But, then, ancient philosophies have been hinting at such things for thousands of years.

2

Dreamworld

What dreaming does is give us the fluidity
to enter into other worlds by destroying
our sense of knowing this world.

- Carlos Castaneda

In life, the closest thing to death that we know (without
actually being dead) is most likely sleep. Scientists have
actually noticed similarities in brainwaves when a person
is sleeping and when they have recently died. That the
brain continues to emit waves after death is fascinating
enough on its own. What is even more intriguing is that
the brain emits similar waves during such occasions as
those seen in dream states.

The truth is scientists still do not know a lot about
sleep, or why we dream. They are not sure how dreams

work, where they come from, let alone how thought and cognition actually manifests within the physiology of the human brain. A number of such experts go on to admit we will probably never know these things for as long as the human race exists, due to its intangible nature. To this day there are neuroscientists, such as Giulio Tononi, who are conducting in-depth research in an attempt to finally decipher the hidden meaning of dreams and varying levels of sleep. Some may call it a last-ditch effort in learning higher insight into the mind's more elusive facets.

The dream state, itself, is a topic of much speculation and the subject of countless studies conducted by scientists and researchers eager to find the hidden meaning behind the mind's rambunctious nature. While theories of why we dream and what it means have come by way of psychologists and scientists, the more subtle connotations still remain beyond our immediate understanding.

Because some states of consciousness, while we sleep, exhibit a striking similarity to having died, a number of researchers have gone far enough to describe sleep as a type of miniature death. Since existence beyond the physical world is explained by some old philosophies as our natural state of existence, it is not surprising we would return to it on a regular basis. We are constantly practicing death through sleep, testing that familiar state from where we came. As studies have shown, those people who claim to be able to project their consciousness out of their body while asleep are actually in a state that resembles death while doing so.

Ancient Egyptians believed the dreamworld was a doorway to the afterlife. They believed dreaming was the only way to truly see the meaning of existence while still in the land of the living. By traveling into the afterlife while in the dream state, ancient Egyptians claimed to be able to bring back knowledge of what they saw. One group, known as the Cult of Osiris—Osiris was an ancient Egyptian king who became known as the god of death and resurrection—would actually seal a man in a casket and count for about eight minutes before letting him out. Nearly suffocating while inside, the person would have a Near Death Experience and then come back (hopefully) to describe what they saw while in the afterlife. It was clear, according to hieroglyphs left on walls and what had been written in Egypt's, *Book of the Dead*, that dreaming was a very important part of Egyptian culture.

Australian Aborigines, a people who have been around for more than 50,000 years, fully believe dreaming is a doorway which allows them to return to the existence they all had before coming into the physical world. The existence experienced in what they call, 'The Dreamtime', is believed to be the true reality. The Dreamtime is nothing less than an opportunity to return to that natural state from which Australian Aborigines—in fact, all of us —come.

Many old and indigenous cultures believe every dream has importance, no matter how frivolous it may seem upon waking. To many, each dream is a journey into an alternate realm of existence that is as real as waking reality. Within this philosophy it is possible to encounter other beings we have known for thousands—possibly even millions—of years. Or we can travel back to the same place over and over, feeling we have known it for ages, even though we may have never been there while awake. Anyone who has experienced a dream where they have encountered someone, or something, and felt overwhelming emotions for what seems like no logical reason can begin to understand how these alternate realities may hold greater meaning than initially understood.

Those who have become fascinated by dreams and who have actually found themselves exploring the full potential of dreaming, know there is far more involved than merely some movie-reel of images that appear to be brought to life through the subconscious. For anyone who has immersed him or herself in dream states, it seems that dreaming offers a level of consciousness we still do not fully understand. Brain waves move onto a plane of activity quite similar to those who have experienced brief periods wherein they have qualified as clinically dead. As we fall asleep and slip further from one level of awareness into another, we flirt with the level of consciousness that seems to be death itself.

The plane of awareness that has been called the 'astral plane' would seem to be the doorway leading to the afterlife. This is what was touted by ancient Egyptians as that which led to a world where the gods actually dwell. The many tales that are recounted by medical patients who have been on the edge of death, their heart still and lifeless on the operating table while doctors and nurses struggle to bring them back, is that of their conscious awareness floating out of their body, coming to rest against the ceiling above as they stare down at the pandemonium below. Their experiences, after having been resuscitated, are commonly described as a profound feeling of well being, along with an indifference to the physical life from which they have briefly become detached. This is sometimes accompanied by visions of light and an indefinable presence that emanates feelings of peace and love. They tell their family and loved ones, after having gone through such an ordeal, that they know there is nothing to fear and that death is not the end. So profound is their experience, usually, that they are changed forever. The world of the living is never the same for them afterward.

All of us apparently do dream. Those who claim to never dream actually do, according to studies; they simply do not remember it. In fact, most people forget their dream by the time they have climbed out of bed. Studies suggest we usually dream three to six times per night and each dream lasts between five and twenty minutes. Some studies point to even higher numbers than that.

This is all fine, but why do we experience dreams?

Dreaming is a state of conscious awareness. When we dream, our consciousness is transformed in such a way that our dreaming existence becomes reality, as far as we perceive it. It is no different than when we wake. Once awake, we find our consciousness has again been transformed. As far as we perceive our waking life, this has now become our true reality.

Some neuroscientists who have studied brain activity have come to believe that consciousness is something that does not really exist within the physiology of the brain. These scientists have theorized that consciousness continues to exist even after the brain has ceased, which could go a long way to explain why brain patterns at certain stages of sleep resemble those of a person who has recently died.

There is a fascinating chemical which is believed the brain secretes when we fall into certain states of sleep, called dimethyltryptamine (DMT). This chemical acts as a powerful hallucinogen who some think may be responsible for producing dreams. Others have come to believe it acts as a doorway that lets us through to the afterlife. What is particularly fascinating is the theory that the brain also produces DMT during death. This has led a number of doctors to conclude that Near Death Experiences are nothing more than a hallucinogenic 'trip' the person has witnessed in the form of a vision. If this is so, the question remains, how could that person be envisioning or dreaming anything while they are supposedly dead (in the clinical sense).

As seems to be the case with many such drugs, DMT has been used in a recreational form. Those studying the affect of DMT on such users find the hallucinations bear a striking similarity from one person to another. Those using DMT as a curiosity report going to the same place as that reported by many other subjects. Users have also described encounters with beings that are strikingly similar to those witnessed from one person to the next. Stories of strange, elf-like creatures, welcoming users to their world and showing them wonders that are hard to appreciably describe through human language, appear to be fairly common.

Some have speculated that these beings may be extra-dimensional entities that exist in a parallel universe to ours. Others believe they may even be deceased people from our world who now exist in another reality. Users of DMT who have encountered these beings often experience an inexplicable familiarity and report an indescribable love toward them that transcends the physical world. Their experience and the worlds they encounter seem more real than physical existence itself. Many can not find words with which to describe the encounter satisfactorily. What is clear is that a large number of users who experience the journey come back completely convinced that this other world, to which they just traveled, actually exists. This is quite different from LSD, mescaline or psilocybin users, who clearly feel their own experience was simply a hallucination. It is not uncommon for the DMT user to come back emotionally impacted beyond explanation and describing their experience as life altering.

Given the evidence that the worlds to which DMT grants us access appear quite similar, perhaps ancient Egyptians were more aware than we know in believing dreams truly are a gateway to the afterlife. At the very least, it appears to be an alternate existence to which dreaming may be the first step in reaching through other levels of consciousness.

If DMT acts as some sort of doorway, it seems many are opening a common door and traveling to the same place.

From the beginning, my own life seems to have been immersed in dreams. At times, my most powerful insights appear to have come from the dream state. It has often seemed that dreams resemble a looking glass back to something that holds a hidden meaning from which we have become detached.

There have been numerous occasions during which I have returned to places in my dreams that are all too familiar, as though they are a home of some sort. Yet, in the waking world I have never been to any of them, or had any inkling of their existence. There are also people I am well acquainted with in dreams. It often feels as though I belong among them more so than I do during my waking reality. I have actually wept with joy upon finding some of those souls in dreams, along with those places I seem to know so well, even though upon waking I realize they have nothing to do with my present existence whatsoever.

I have heard tales of some people experiencing repetitive dreams, but such experiences are usually disturbing to the dreamer. From my own point of view, I find the repetition and familiarity comforting and a welcome respite. I have also walked in the land of dreams, knowing full well they are dreams—what is known as a 'lucid dream'. Being aware of this altered state of consciousness actually allows the dreamer to manipulate the world around them, given they have the mental capacity to do so.

Because dreams can be so emotionally empowering, I have always thought there was far more to them than being mere reflections of our subconscious thought, as some psychologists have suggested.

Lucid dreams are said to be a gateway into yet another state of consciousness referred to as the astral plane. Astral projection is said to be a way to move from our physical body into a reality beyond.

My latest encounters with the astral plane have occurred during those rare, waking moments wherein I was still essentially dreaming, but woke briefly from the dream. It has usually been on those occasions, wherein I have allowed myself to sink back into sleep, that I have had the greatest success at manipulating the dreamworld by remaining lucid. During a particular instance, I decided I would try to leave my body, rather than indulge myself in the usual luxuries of simply creating and manipulating the lucid dream.

I actually felt myself slip freely—quite abruptly—from my physical body as it lay on the bed. While doing this, I made a conscious effort not to float to the ceiling, as is usually the experience among reported cases. Instead, I tried to keep myself low to the ground, just to see if there was a difference from the many recited, cliché scenarios.

It turned out there was a substantial effect in this simple act. Instead of feeling the detached sensation of contentment I had been accustomed to hearing from others, I felt an overpowering sense of foreboding. I clearly felt as though I were not the only one there in the room. In fact, I could distinctly sense there were other presences all around me. Dread flowed in as if a floodgate had opened.

I quickly retreated into my body and woke up. The awareness of something being there beyond myself was markedly similar, though much more pronounced, to what I used to feel after spending months meditating in order to transcend the world around me. Even as I existed there on the astral plane sensing that presence, I realized I could discover it more thoroughly by simply allowing myself to sink further into that state.

During astral projection, the sensation of moving from the physical body into a realm beyond is strange, to say the least, if not unnerving. It feels unsettling and empowering at the same time. Contradictorily, this strange sensation is also familiar in a way, as if it is something we have experienced many times in the past. Could it be the experience feels natural simply because the sensation is a characteristic of how we commonly navigate between death and life without a sense of distance? It is as if distance really has no meaning. In the astral world, which seems to be a type of dream state as we can best describe it, things can be made to happen instantaneously. It has been taught by skilled practitioners that the universe can be traversed by mere thought, taking us to where we wish within the blink of an eye. Just as we can jump instantly from one realm to an entirely different one while experiencing a lucid dream, the same is possible during astral projection.

Such physically defying feats could never be experienced within our waking reality. Or could they? Science has forecast such instantaneous voyages as possible and within the realm of physics. We simply lack the current technology to enable it, though it is predicted that one day the technology will exist. So, could such voyages be out of the question within separate planes of consciousness?

The physical world, as we understand it, simply does not exist in higher realities. This is the reason such instantaneous journeys and transitions are possible on the astral plane. Perhaps one of the reasons most of us seem unable to remember our past existence in an alternate reality is because our mind, anchored here in the physical world, could simply not comprehend such an existence. If we did truly remember that existence, it could likely drive us to great conflict while here in this one.

Indeed, in the dreamworld things which seem absolutely ludicrous and defiant of logic upon waking seem completely natural at the time we experience them. This would appear to be due to our conscious awareness moving into a different reality while operating at a level we rarely experience during waking moments. To exist in a dreamworld, or to move about on the astral plane, our level of awareness must transform to adapt to that place. This is why seemingly bizarre experiences in dream states appear to make perfect sense at the time we are dreaming. A different level of our consciousness has taken over and is guiding us through the dreamworld, so we can exist there without conflict to what we have grown to understand in the waking world.

Behind the veil of physical diversion exists countless planes where past, present and future all exist at the same time. Of those planes are many parallels of existence. Even the study of physics has suggested such far flung theories as being quite possible. For many of us, though, it is still difficult to comprehend.

For some, dreams are events that have already happened, or are going to happen some time in the future. Perhaps they are both. If dreams are doorways to other realms of existence and consciousness, we could be traveling through all of them at any given moment, past, present and future.

Our perception of time is clearly altered during dream states. There are times, while dreaming, when it seems a lifetime is passing. Upon waking, we realize it could only have been a matter of minutes, especially if we take note of the time before we start dreaming and when we wake from that dream. Sleep researchers find there is only a small percentage of time wherein we actually do dream, as the remaining hours are spent falling into different levels of consciousness while asleep.

As a child I had many vivid nightmares which largely involved my being among things in this world I would normally take for granted. I would be in a fairly average room full of people and everything would seem to be as it should. However, something would usually happen to disrupt that perception. One person in the room, sitting on a couch between several other people, would catch my attention. There would be something I felt was wrong about that one person; something that would frighten me. Naturally, I would approach the person and look at them more closely. Sometimes I would even engage them in conversation, but I would always know as soon as I began to speak to them that something was not right. They simply did not belong in my present reality. Simply peering at them I would usually know it, even though they would look like everyone else.

It was not until I would do something more forward, such as touch their hand, that I would realize they were not actually human like the others in the room. They were something inexplicable and disturbing. Sometimes to make the point clear, their features would immediately change so I would clearly know they were out of place. What a moment ago was a man was now suddenly part bird, or some other insane, nonsensical being. The face, which was that of a human, would quickly become the face of a strange animal with a beak or hairy snout. Likewise, the hand I was shaking would become a claw or talon.

This sounds amusing as I recite it, but the experience would be quite vivid and evoke great anxiety. I would invariably wake up in a cold sweat, panicked and my heart pounding.

Later in life, I would find this sort of dream is common among many people. In fact, ancient philosophies are riddled with folklore of our existence among other beings who are represented as part human and part beast

It was not until later when I matured somewhat that I began to think these events were not simple, illogical nightmares, but more a way my psyche was trying to make sense of the world into which I had recently been thrust. I was still dealing with the sudden change in realities, from the one in which I had existed before to the one where I now found myself. As time went by and I began to accept my new existence more fully, the nightmares became fewer and less frequent.

It seems only when we are young and still carry the memories of our prior existence in a world that is far different from the one in which we now find ourselves, our subconscious struggles with images that seem maddening and irrational. As we become more adjusted and lose our hold on what we were before our physical life, dreams usually fade from the truly bizarre to things that make more sense to us. This could be because we have assimilated to the physical world and believe it more as years go by. I do admit, however, to still having dreams that are more bizarre than most people's my age.

Recently, I had a lucid dream wherein I was sure all the other participants were completely unaware they were part of the dream. I tried to convince them they were all dreaming, but I seemed to be the only one who was aware of it. To prove my point I consciously changed the physical structure of the dreamworld, creating tiny objects out of nothing and forcing them to float up into the air around us. With this, the other participants immediately became convinced their world truly was nothing more than illusion. Just as we were planning our revolt against the dreamworld, it all came to an end and I woke up.

TRANSFORMATION

In many old cultures there would be a clear belief that the place and the people within that dream actually exist, but simply within another reality.

It is interesting that we all appear to have similar dreams; dreams which psychologists take great effort to dissect and analyze. From Sigmund Freud to Carl Jung, there are many hidden meanings read into dreams and what they could mean. It is quite like a caveman trying to describe what a modern jetliner crossing the sky above could possibly signify. In his limited understanding, the airplane must be some manifestation from the heavens, the sun, or whatever god he chooses to worship. Contemporary psychiatrists and mental wizards can be thought of in much the same way. Such disciples of the mind do their best to hand down their interpretations in an attempt to bring reason to the irrational.

Perhaps the answer is as simple as realizing we all dream the same things because we are all the same being and of the same overall consciousness. We are equally aware and remember similar things from our prior existence and manifest them in our dreams the same way. I could go so far to say all of us are returning to the same ethereal existence from which we came, each time we close our eyes and fall asleep.

Tibetan monks believe that after life we revert back to the Bardo, which is a realm of disembodied consciousness that exists immediately following death where the spirit dwells before embarking on its next journey. It is said this post-death existence is very much like a dream state. Believers and practitioners of astral projection also see this journey into the afterlife as being similar to a dream.

Dreamworld

There is a powerful familiarity in the dream state, as though part of our consciousness has always belonged there. Perhaps it gives a subtle solace in the physical world where we dwell before death.

I have had a dream where I find myself in a small town, not far from where I live today. As I walked about the town, I began to encounter other people within it. Even though upon waking I realized I had never met those same people in my waking life, in the dream I realized I had come upon them many times in the past. It could very well be I have always known them in another reality, as some philosophies suggest.

In my dream, these people would eventually disappear into the town and I would follow. They would soon elude me and as I became more frantic to find them, I realized I was reconstructing the town as I searched for them. Soon I became lost because the town was no longer what I had initially realized it to be.

I have done the same thing many times after falling into a lucid dream, seeing clearly where I was; not awake, but sleeping. I have then taken a god-like approach in constructing the dream as I wander through it.

Recently, I experienced a lucid dream wherein I knew full well I was dreaming, just like any other. On this occasion, however, I stopped long enough to take the time to examine the reality around me. Knowing I was dreaming, I felt I should have been able to tell the difference between the dream and my waking reality with ease. The truly remarkable thing is that even though I was completely aware I was dreaming, the more I scrutinized the dreamworld around me and peered closely at its fabric, the more real it became. It actually became more real than my waking reality, which I found to be absolutely incredible.

This is what is so fascinating. Even though I knew the dream was just that, I was unable to expose it as any less real than anything else I knew. It simply became more real, felt more substantial and increased in detail as I did my best to poke holes in its very substance. This is why I believe so strongly that reality is based completely on perception. Even when I felt convinced my reality was illusion, it seemed every bit as vivid—even more so—as my waking reality!

The transformation of our mind determines what is real. Once perception engulfs what we accept as reality, there is no more illusion as far as our personal point of view is concerned.

Even during a lucid dream, there have been times I would lose myself within it, forgetting where I was and soon becoming another oblivious wanderer. The dream takes over and soon I am at the mercy of my subconscious once more.

This is how it is when we are born into the physical world. Life is another dream of which we are either aware, or in which we completely lose ourselves and forget everything else we once knew before that moment. This is why being born is very much the same as falling asleep. It is one state of consciousness that moves into another. This is probably why so many older cultures who remember their experience of prior existence and physical birth see such similarity in dreaming while alive in the world.

I have had another lucid dream wherein I wander about

an elaborate city that seems to go on forever. The city is beautiful. I encounter people within it who, again, I apparently know. Something about the city sparkles and shimmers. I look closely at the walls and realize they have a myriad system of transparent veins running through them. Blood does not pump through the veins however. Instead of blood, the veins are filled with pure energy and light. The city is actually alive, but not in the way we know. It is alive with pure thought. Even though I am aware I am dreaming, the experience captivates me and pulls me in further.

There are sometimes signs in our dream which should have the power to wake us to realizing we are dreaming.

I recently had a dream in which I knew something was not quite right and to which I should have been paying attention. There were undulating rivers flowing through the streets of a city in which I wandered and which teemed with Antarctic life—seals and killer whales. This was odd as it was a hot, sunny day. Those same swelling rivers flowed into highway interchanges that became impossible for motorcars to bypass. Beyond them were waterfalls, up which tourists would swim against the natural pull of gravity, only to finally be cast down again at the verge of reaching the top. Upon closer inspection, I realized the rivers were not even water but actually consisted of large, white spheres that toppled over the swimmers like a frothy foam. The spheres moved with a great force and buoyancy beyond the known laws of physics.

Things like these should have indicated I was somewhere beyond my waking reality. Deep down, I believe I was aware of it. It also seemed as though I should have been there and that I should have accepted the seemingly conflicting order of things. My consciousness had simply been transformed to a point where this was now an acceptable reality.

We question which one is the real world. After we wake, that always seems to be the one that is true. However, while in the dream it usually seems *that* is the true reality. The matter of perception remains a translation of our mind that science has yet to unravel. When we wake from the dreamworld we say to ourselves, "Ah yes, I remember this is the real world". This could be simply because places and people repeat their existence over and over. It is like a constant re-emphasis of what we interpret as being true reality. While in the dreamworld, however, those of us who go to the same place with the same people could easily argue that very point. Which reality is true?

The difference between sleeping and waking reality is that even though each may seem equally valid, we are not usually aware of waking realities while we dream (unless we are in a lucid dream, but even then we do not usually think beyond what is presently happening). We do know we have had a dream while in our waking reality, however. In contrast, the dreaming reality is so overpowering that we are no longer aware of our waking world. The dream becomes all that exists for us. Perhaps this is because our consciousness if free to drift to any level, far beyond our physical reality. While awake, we are trapped with limited means. Through death, many of us also lose our sense of the physical world, just as we do through dreaming.

The question of which one is the true reality could come down to a simple answer—both are equally real. It is simply that we live in an altered state in both worlds, perhaps neither one being any less real than the other.

They simply exist in differing terms.

Ancient Egyptians were certainly not the only culture that believed dreams were a passage to the afterlife. There is evidence that ancient Rome and Greece held similar beliefs. Many ancient civilizations, which have vanished from this earth, have left evidence of their belief that dreams are a way to return to our natural and eternal state of being. I believe, eventually, we all become self-realizing, at which point the exercise of living a physical life becomes moot.

It is amazing that we have the power to shape and form our own dreams. We can actually use them to propel ourselves toward greater awakening. Yet, some of us never seem to realize this for what it offers. I think this could be because many of us still fear our dreams, simply because we do not understand them. We are a long way from knowing what the human mind really is and how it is connected to conscious awareness. There seems to be a vast gap between Eastern and Western cultures, the latter of which is still vastly immature when compared to the former, especially were consciousness is concerned.

We continue to jump back and forth from one state of conscious awareness to another. Perhaps we are only allowed snippets of our alternate reality for as long as we are physically alive, until then waiting for our time to return to the dreamworld for good.

Often, I have thought dreams are not merely unresolved issues that are working their way through our subconscious, as so many psychologists would intone. Instead, I think they are projections of something locked away inside us.

TRANSFORMATION

The idea that our waking reality is actually an illusion, projected from some hidden place beyond our known universe, offers a unique parallel and begins to explain things we have suspected but could not previously prove.

A theory that has been gaining popularity among some of the foremost respected physicists of our world is the Holographic Universe Theory. Already, mathematics strongly argues the possibility of the theory, much like equations proved Einstein's Special Theory of Relativity before the technology existed to physically test it. It was years after the fact that we were able to physically prove the theory of relativity by comparing two atomic clocks, one in motion on a jet airplane and one standing still. As forecast by the mathematical formulas, the clock on the airplane moved more slowly than the stationary one. In fact, an experiment has already taken place in order to substantiate the existence of the holographic universe, but with inconclusive results. So far it is neither proved or disproved. Being a fairly new theory—it was only proposed in 1993 by Dutch Physicist, Gerard 't Hooft—it will take some time before we become more acquainted with its possibilities.

In a nutshell, the holographic universe theory implies we do not actually exist in the form we have come to accept as our reality. Instead, the holographic universe posits we exist somewhere outside our known 3-dimensional reality and that everything in our universe, along with ourselves, is an illusion being projected from some point beyond what we see. The theory derives much of its science from Stephen Hawking's revelations in black hole physics. It has been discussed and written by such renown physicists as Brian Greene, Juan Maldacena and

Leonard Susskind (who is largely responsible for advancing the theory), to name a few.

In part two of this book I will go into a bit more detail of exactly what the holographic universe theory entails.

That our entire existence could actually be projected from some other point in space and time, whether in this reality or another, offers some intriguing possibilities. We may all actually be projecting ourselves from some other dimension in quite the same way we project ourselves in dream states. Just as some claim the dreamworld is nothing more than illusion, the ramifications of the holographic universe suggest our waking reality may be as equally illusory.

Could it be our physical awareness is simply another form of lucid dreaming?

Quantum mechanics has already shown some of the particles that make up our world remain in a subjective state. These particles and their existence have been revealed to exist in a certain form only for as long as we observe them. What this might suggest is that the nature of our universe may simply appear to exist in its present form due to our collective consciousness. In a very real sense, it is our conscious awareness that is creating our very own reality. This is something ancient Hindu philosophies have been saying for centuries. If we did not exist, the universe might very well not exist either. We could be projecting our very own reality into a form we simply accept as real.

The entire concept of a holographic universe also opens up the likelihood of higher dimensions and alternate levels of existence.

Ancient Egyptians believed the dream state as being a gateway into another reality. Given the holographic universe theory, those beliefs could find a basis in fact. Astral projection could very well be as real as the projections we experience through the holographic universe. Anyone who has practiced astral projection will swear it is completely real; never mind that they may have never even heard of a holographic reality.

What a revelation it would be to have our waking existence validated as being just as much an illusion as our dreams.

The field of psychology does what it can in an effort to interpret dreams, guessing from where they come in order to pacify popular confusion. The problem is there is no quantifiable way to measure a dream. Due to this lack of hard science, any hope of adequately deciphering the meaning of dreams is potentially lost forever.

Scientists and researchers explain dreaming as a necessary function for the development and evolution of the human psyche. Yet, many of us, as we become more engulfed by the pressing urgency of life, put thoughts of dreams as far to the back of our mind as possible. It could be that many of us simply can not remember a dream from the time we wake and make it to the bathroom solely because we see it as a useless and confusing function that holds no importance. Contrast this with our ancient ancestors and their staunch commitment to embracing the dreamworld for the sake of their spiritual development.

3

Universal Consciousness

Everything you can imagine is real.

- Pablo Picasso

As bizarre as the simplest answer may be, it could be easier to accept the reason for so many odd occurrences through our seemingly ordinary lives may be due to an unseen, interconnectedness. Even as strange as such a possibility may be, our very existence may be even stranger. If life is truly a dream, it looks as though many of us are dreaming the same dream.

Physics appears to be the great prognosticator, taking the place of what used to be the religious benefactors of our existence. What was once a fanciful and self-indulgent notion, with no way to prove (or disprove) it, is now hard science, at least for now.

TRANSFORMATION

As we learn the deeper subtleties of our world on all its levels, existence becomes more a construct of our creative imagination. Not only may life be a self-designed creation of our own mind, but death may be just as much an illusion as everything else we create through our conscious projection. It seems ironic that as more people become secular and dismissive of creationism, cutting-edge physicists find more evidence that life may be more spiritual than previously thought.

Just as dreams and perception enhancers (such as DMT) open up limitless possibilities for anyone eager to explore the mystical nuances of the mind, the more advanced we become in science, the more accepting we are of whatever we deem possible. As long as there is a scientific excuse for the existence of higher dimensions and parallel universes, we see these as more plausible than such esoteric notions as a Supreme Being. To anything beyond our understanding which can be scientifically excused for its audaciousness, we keep ourselves receptive to possibility.

Yet, it remains the more grandiose presumption that all of us are of a higher awareness and consciously connected to one another that keeps us at bay whenever we hear stirrings of such postulations.

If life is truly an illusion, which keeps us separated from one another, why can we not take the next leap in realizing everything is as much an altered perception as every dream we have? Can we not accept that every dream is just as real as every waking moment we live? Life is cognition, after all. What we accept as real here in the physical world, many of our fellow animals and insects see that same reality in a completely different way. As any honeybee will admit, other forms of life see their existence and the world around them from a completely different perspective than we. Science gives each of us the exact thing we need to survive within our own environment, but only to the point that it makes enough sense to us.

How we perceive our world is completely different from many other animals. We see things as we need to in order to thrive, just as insects experience the same world from an alternate point of view in order that they are able to best survive. Some insects, birds and reptiles see the world not just through color but also through ultraviolet light, giving them a greater sense of detail and allowing them to be receptive to things we are not. All creatures experience their environment in their own way, so reality for one is not necessarily the same for another.

With all these senses and varying means of perceiving our reality, could it be we also have the means to see things beyond our own, presumed abilities?

This is what a fair percentage of us seem to believe. The idea that if other creatures of our wild kingdom are able to see the world beyond another animal's ability, perhaps we also have the means to see things beyond what is immediately obvious. After all, every one of us seems to have the skill to use intuition in order to perceive things beyond our five, physical senses. Sometimes it is nothing more than a feeling that allows us to interact with our world in a way that transcends mere physical ability.

Some of us appear desperate, at times, to declare such notions as extrasensory perception (ESP) to be real. It would, doubtless, be a breakthrough discovery to find that ESP actually exists. After all, it would mean what we perceive as our existence is just a sliver of reality. The verifiable truth of ESP would suggest we are all, indeed, nothing more than mollusks living a confined existence with only a faint knowledge of what we have always suspected to exist beyond physical limit. If we were to discover ourselves to be merely passing travelers who briefly use our physical bodies to get from point A to point B—to find we are far beyond that generalized interpretation—our society would likely collapse under the weight of its own awakening.

Realizing we may have the power to read each others' thoughts, while at the same time influencing one another through mere will, could be a horrific proposition. We might generally play with notions of ESP but the reality is that none of us, secretively, would wish to confront it. How could we exist and continue through life, constantly worrying that others could be invading our mind and spying on our deepest thoughts? These are all things that were never meant to exist in our world. Our reality, after all, requires simplicity. As much as our meager existence is able to persist through total ignorance, the evolution of our various cultures demands the same.

Perhaps in another, much higher state of consciousness, we can indulge such prospects. For now, we simply do not have that luxury. We are already dealing with enough problems of our own doing without 'superpowers' to make things even more complicated. It is probably for the best that we do not have any sort of penchant for higher knowledge beyond what we can use to merely survive our immediate world.

For the most part, science and quantifiable studies have shown there is little evidence that any of us possess the power to dramatically change our environment through no less than pure, mental will. There have been pretenders—Uri Geller is probably one of the most famous professed psychics, being a throwback to the CIA's failed experiments of the 1970s—who have claimed to possess superpowers beyond reckoning. During tests and measured studies, however, these self-proclaimed wizards of the psyche have fallen far short of their majestic affirmations.

Despite this exposure, there remains a loyal following that continues to believe wholeheartedly in parapsychology. Such fanaticism comes in the face of empirical evidence to the contrary. There are those who are committed to their cause, often having personal experiences that defy the measurable evidence that would dismiss psychic events.

While the more wild claims have largely been debunked through simple science, there does remain a small component of paranormal phenomenon that deserves a degree of scrutiny. It is this portion of the bizarre that has kept us from outright denying such vagaries in perception and reality. As long as there are aspects that point toward the psychological probabilities, we can not completely discount every aspect of the paranormal.

Everything we take to be reality requires a certain balance. Even if we have a full capacity for higher power, such as those that have been claimed to exist within the realm of psychic phenomenon, it may be quite counterproductive to our present existence. Imagine a hoard of adolescent Homo sapiens running amok through the streets of our cultivated cities, wreaking havoc on one another simply to exact a crude type of vengeance over the slightest variance in whatever beliefs we may harbor. We have already seen how much destruction comes about simply through ideological difference. If we all had superpowers, it would likely not take us long to wipe each other from the face of the earth, rather than taking the long route of trying to convert everyone else in the world to our own way of thinking.

Still, we continue to hear murmurs of psychic possibilities. The evidence does not come cascading down on us; not to the point where it completely revolutionizes our way of thinking and forces us to embrace a new order. Proclaimed evidence comes in subtle form, as if there exists a consensus that most of us would not want to see the proof to such a mesmerizing discovery.

But, the other side of reality continues to walk a parallel path, constantly hinting there is more than what meets the eye. We hear those whispers in various forms. We may hear it in our dreams or through near death experiences. Then again, maybe our pets are the ones trying to tell us that clairvoyance is real and we should pay attention.

There is still something in our lives, within our world and amongst our reality, that is sometimes more than ordinary.

Everything to do with reality is life, as much as it is death. Once we realize this, all things that contradict our existence become the very essence of our being. We exist in scattered moments, burning up minutes and hours, even millennia, just for the sake of passing time. Everything to do with our concept of time is nothing more than ideological pandering to everything we pretend to know while knowing nothing at all.

Creatures of habit and hope beyond reason, we

continue to believe and struggle while doing our best to ascend. The world has no patience for self-indulgence. Still, there is that everlasting murmur. Every night we go to sleep we continue to hear it, only to soon forget it the very next day.

It is forgotten and, at the same time, never truly forgotten at all.

Life before life and life after death, and all the various incarnations of those prospects, seem to be largely wrapped up among such other variances as parapsychology. The pundits continue to claim that if one exists then surely the other must equally exist.

Many of these notions should not be taken as a conglomerate assumption, simply for lack of knowledge. The idea that we continue to exist after death, and before even being born into life, should not be blindly accepted as a rationalized conclusion that all things otherworldly simply exist for the sake of one another. That we exist and always have does not necessarily mean suddenly we can bend spoons with our mind.

Life and eternal existence is far more significant and beyond our scope of physical understanding than mere parlor tricks that suggest the realization of one does not mean all things are without reproach. If we are to exist here, the same laws apply as those that would to any of our lesser animal brothers within the same world of experience. In order to keep all things equal, we simply need to adhere to a world of clearly understood physical laws.

In keeping with our infinitely curious nature, it would be inevitable we would continue to seek out and find new challenges that may defy our understanding of existence. Hence, the creation of quantum mechanics. If ever we needed a set of laws that could explain the inexplicable contradictions of our physical nature, it is most certainly the advent of quantum theory, along with all the bizarre uncertainty that comes with it.

It may seem our existence is woven into the fabric of plausibility. Anyone who has studied the peculiar nature of quantum mechanics soon discovers things exist as a matter of probability. In a world of physics and science, where empirically qualifying everything is the key to our physical reality, how can it be the implications are that we may exist, or we may not, depending on whether we are consciously aware of it at any given moment?

This is the reality of our ever expanding base of knowledge. The more we discover previously unrealized levels of reality and existence, the more we find everything we thought up to that point may have been deeply flawed. Just as we seem to have come to grips with reality and physics, the latest level of our understanding of the physical world reveals we really know nothing at all. The more we learn, the more it becomes evident we still have much further to go. The truth may be that for as long as we exist in the physical world we may never truly understand what is actually real.

All this may be due to the simple fact we view our reality from an imperfect perspective. We see our reality from the point of view of a finite, physical brain that interfaces with our world on a limited scale. Just as every other living creature on our planet sees things from their own perspective, we do the same. None of us are actually seeing our reality for what it truly is (whatever that may be). It appears completely reasonable to say all reality is completely subjective, thus lacking validity.

If we stop and think of reality as a certain set of laws and nothing more, we have already locked ourselves up with no chance for higher insight.

Famous psychics used to insist they could move objects with nothing more than a thought. Within the world of parapsychology, this is termed as psychokinesis. As much as our intelligence community, encompassed by such branches with acronyms like CIA , NSA and DIA, has largely dispelled such exotic claims, there remain adherents who insist they can perform such miraculous feats.

Other purported powers include such things as psychic surgery (the removal of a disease or physical disorder through laying hands on the body) and remote viewing (seeing what someone is doing on the other side of the world by simply imagining it).

Such powers and declarations are clearly bold and daring. Those self-claimed talents of individuals such as Uri Geller, along with the ability of some to bend spoons with nothing more than their mind, have largely been exposed as parlor tricks. Despite assertions and dramatic exhibitions to convince the public such powers are real, there remains a small area of psychic phenomenon that has not been completely dismissed. Even those individuals who measure and quantify claims of precognition and telepathy do not seem to be categorically denying the possibility of these last two examples. It is these ones in particular that seem to indicate that intuition may actually hold some solid ground within the realm of the possible.

The strange thing about precognition or clairvoyance is

that the whole idea seems so lost in fantasy and popular movies that most of us can not even begin to accept such extravagant concepts. What is most interesting, however, is there seems to be an abundance of examples from people who exist in every walk of life. Such people may not even subscribe to these ideas, but have had experiences nevertheless.

Any psychic phenomenon that may have given the West, or the East, a leg up during the Cold War was never discounted and was actively explored as a possible weapon to use against global adversaries. Considering mythical tales of the past and purported instances through history, wherein prophets and oracles were alleged to merely be human beings with the power of second sight, it is no wonder our intelligence agencies were once eager to exploit such possibilities.

Perhaps it is an inevitable conclusion that scientific studies were never able to prove the existence of any psychic phenomenon that was considered viable as an active weapon. If psychic ability is anything that should be considered divine, it is probably not the lot of mankind to employ it as a tool of selfish intent to be used against one another.

As far as the scientific mind is concerned, there can be no logical explanation for even considering parapsychology as a legitimate field of study. Yet, the Central Intelligence Agency spent years researching it in an attempt to cultivate the phenomenon into a viable means of spying on their political enemies. The phenomenon of ESP was actively pursued as a potential weapon against America's enemy, whether it was Russia, China, or the communist East in Europe at the time. (From what we know, during the Cold War the other side was also involved in exploiting such areas of diabolical pseudoscience.)

Alas, the CIA program (under the colorful codename, Star Gate) was terminated and declassified in 1995, citing that no conclusive evidence had been found to support it actually worked.

However, the idea that the mind might see things that our eyes can not, or are unable to interpret through any of our other five senses, becomes intriguing. The possibility we can sense things through a medium as esoteric as mere thought provokes impatience in some, as they scoff at the apparent absurdity. Still, others find such prospects fascinating, as well as encouraging.

It may be a delightful revelation to find we possess suppressed abilities to sense the world around us through a higher means than merely the physical. Such a discovery could suggest we are all connected through the fabric of the universe; even the very fabric of existence. Perhaps we are not as isolated from one another as commonly thought. It would also mean we are all very much the same, free to communicate with one another and equally open to influence.

For the most part, I have discounted much of ESP as a passing fancy. Since the verdict is largely still out on whether there is truly anything to it, the doorway remains open to colorful interpretations. What better medium could there be, after all, to claim a handle over powers that are difficult to prove, or otherwise disprove. It is no wonder certain individuals still exist among us who derive monetary favors from other people's desperation for an answer beyond what they are capable of glimmering on their own. That there are those who use such hazy areas to their advantage in order to solicit wealth has surely done little to help support the argument that ESP, in any form, may be legitimate.

As mentioned above, those many negative incarnations of what may, or could, be does not necessarily preclude everything outright. To this day, I still believe there is a higher medium beyond our immediate awareness that allows us to communicate and see things in terms beyond what we may call a physical explanation. What some would call coincidence may be more than such a simple interpretation. It could be that what we might describe as a universal consciousness may explain the more intangible aspects of our own reality. Of all the variations of ESP I have explored, there appears little evidence except that one abstract concept that seems to bind us all together. This is where such notions as precognition, astral projection and telepathy may actually hold some legitimacy beyond the latest science fiction thriller at your local movie theater.

First Signs

How I came about my suspicion that telepathy and clairvoyance may actually hold some validity evolved through an unusual circumstance. For some reason—one I can not fully recount—I ended up in a detention hall one day while in high school. There was also a particular classmate who found his way to the same place during that offhand occasion.

Quite bored, I proposed some simple experiments to

my fellow detainee in order to pass the time. I am not too sure why—possibly popular impressions of the time—but I had an urge to test the whole clairvoyance thing. To my surprise, I found the impromptu experiment to be quickly yielding, not just for myself but also for my fellow delinquent.

I told him to think of a number between one and ten. More than that, I told him to concentrate on the number and make an image of it in his head. Thinking back, it was quite reminiscent of some hokey magic act; probably the result of watching too many television episodes of *The Magician*, starring Bill Bixby.

The surprising result was that six to seven times out of ten my classmate would guess the actual number I was thinking about. It was even more bizarre when we changed roles and I would guess the number on which my classmate was concentrating with a similar rate of success.

After researching the same sort of experiments conducted under similar situations many years after this, I discovered our results were quite extraordinary. While we conducted these experiments, I could actually see the number come to mind. The key appeared to simply clear the head of all thought and wait for an impression to come on its own. I found that if I waited longer after my initial impression and another number came to mind, it would usually be wrong. So, what I learned was that the first impression I saw in my head was usually the right one. Waiting longer seemed to allow my friend's mind to wander, which would allow other numbers to come into thought.

There were also some occasions wherein I could see my friend was not taking things seriously, during which I would not get an immediate impression of anything.

I was actually quite stunned by all this. In fact, that simple experiment would only be part of a lifetime of experiences that would change my view of the physical world and psychic phenomenon. Many things would happen to me following this incident that would be even more stunning.

When I was younger, I had inklings of similar experiences. All have become so reinforcing that I am now quite convinced that the world, our lives and what we understand as our universe, are all tied together in a very real way that allows us insight into our existence.

Long before the above experience, I had felt there was something that enabled us to sense and understand one another on a completely different level; something that had nothing to do with verbal communication.

One of my earliest thoughts, while still quite young, was how strange I found it that we all communicate with one another by making sounds from our throat. I was taught, just as we are all taught from the moment we are able to understand, that we must make auditory noises in order to communicate and be understood. The moment I realized this was how we communicate in life, I had even more reason to doubt my reality. Such a way to communicate simply did not seem natural. I later realized this imperfect means of expression was why we are so fraught with misunderstanding and the various innuendos that lead to misplaced resentment.

It sounds strange as I write this, but human vocalizations were always very odd to me while growing up. Now that I am older and have nestled into my place in the world, I simply accept it in the same way we all do.

As I lay helpless in that hospital crib on the night of my birth, I remained struck by the savagery of our physical bodies, from breathing air to swallowing oral secretions. Unable to understand each other until we learn to make sounds and hurl them at one another is just another distortion of reality. It is only at a certain point wherein we find ourselves elevated beyond those meager limitations of our new lives that we are eventually able to look beyond what we are and how we truly see ourselves. We all appear to be tied to one another, despite our religion, despite our language and despite our culture. Many of us go through life denying these sensations, but the reality is that we are all the same beings, born from the same mix and, in essence, all the same souls.

The universe seems to constantly whisper to us. Some may describe that as clairvoyance, but I choose to call it connectivity. It is the ultimate connectivity and it exists beyond our physical condition.

I remember a particular night when my fiance and I were preparing for our upcoming wedding. My mother was flying from the West coast to spend the week with us while we prepared for our gala event. Since we had spent a year saving our money to pay for everything, we were quite excited to have all our family come and marvel at our mad and youthful orchestrations.

The night before my mother was due to arrive, we were just getting back home after having gone out for dinner. The sky was clear and the stars were out in force. As we approached the front door of the house, I heard a noise and gazed up. Directly above us, a jet airliner was flying high overhead.

TRANSFORMATION

In the moment I saw the plane flying through the evening sky I was seized with an overwhelming sense of dread. I stopped dead in my tracks as I stared at the blinking lights of the plane.

When my fiance asked what was the matter, I told her I had an undeniable feeling there was going to be a terrible plane crash. It was nothing as concrete as a voice speaking directly to me and warning of some impending doom. If it had, I would have checked myself into the nearest asylum. The sensation was one of just knowing, within a split second, that something awful was going to happen.

For the rest of the night, I went on about the plane crash, rationalizing that perhaps it may have been some sort of premonition of my mother's jet going down in a fiery blaze. After all, she was flying out to be with us that very night so I merely assumed the sense of impending doom may have been connected to her flight. It was also not the first time I had experienced similar feelings of dread, only to see them come true.

Fortunately, I found out the next day my mother had arrived safely at the airport. After spending the day visiting my aunt and uncle, she arrived at our house and we were soon immersed in wedding plans. We talked about flowers, the various guests and looked at seating arrangements, discussing which people should be seated with one another. Around the time we nearly had all the seating figured out, except for one last table, the telephone rang and my fiance answered it. Her father was on the other end.

"Do you see what's happening?" he asked her.

She was not quite sure what he meant.

"Are you watching the TV?" he went on. "You'd

better turn on the TV right away!"

She hung up the phone and went to the television, explaining the brief, somewhat cryptic conversation she just had with her father.

It did not matter to which channel we tuned the television, all of them were broadcasting the same footage. Every station had a graphic scene of the World Trade Center, along with a huge column of smoke billowing from what appeared to be a rather large hole in the side of one of the twin towers.

A voice came on explaining that no one was sure whether the plane had crashed accidentally, let alone *why* it had crashed. The voice then declared, rather excitedly, that a second airplane seemed to be approaching the South Tower. In that moment, it was clear that an airplane had hit the North Tower first. Then, we saw a second airplane flying straight toward the other building and it became horrifyingly apparent it was about to crash into the opposite tower.

We were frozen in place as we watched the fireball erupt as the second plane slammed into the South Tower. The image of the impacting plane and the building erupting in flame was surreal, to say the least. We probably all had the same feeling—this could not possibly be happening and we must be watching some sort of movie. The entire scenario seemed more like something from a Bruce Willis action film, rather than the reality that was unfolding before us.

Far too quickly, the realization of what was taking place seemed to break us from our trance.

The World Trade Center attack sufficiently diverted us from our wedding plans and I think it may have even been the next day when the realization finally hit me.

"My God," I said to my fiance. "Remember the night we came back from dinner and I had that feeling there was going to be a terrible plane crash?"

Clearly due to the shock and impact of the catastrophe, it took that long for me to realize what had happened and to put the two events together.

Such an overwhelming tragedy must have sent some sort of ripple through space and time, I later reasoned. Could such an aberration exist, causing me to sense it before it even happened?

Time, reality and existence are all strange concepts. Perhaps the above event had already happened in a different reality. Maybe it had occurred on another time line and we were simply living through it again.

Before you say, "what the heck is he talking about?" let us consider something. New concepts in time definition depict the past, future and present as existing within the same space at the same moment, but merely on a different line than the one we may be on at any given moment. The possibility that precognition is not so much seeing into the future as it is remembering events that have already transpired in another reality could make such anomalies more possible to substantiate. That the past, present and future may all exist in the same space at once is a mind-bending concept. It has also become a very contentious proposition put forth by some reputable physicists, such as Brian Greene, as well as Dr. Michio Kaku, who has explored the possibilities in a number of his popularized best-selling books on theoretical physics.

What may seem a possible explanation is drawn from our current theories in physics that offer the prospect that we should not treat time as a flowing stream which moves only in one direction. Unlike traditional theories, wherein we previously imagined it as a constantly moving point, physicists are now seeing time as a static event, wherein the past, present and future all exist within the same space. Thinking of the concept in such a way turns the model of time into one that is circular, rather than linear. The theory holds some validity and comes by way of Einstein's revelation of seeing time as another way of describing 3-dimensional space. It is a fascinating concept that I describe in some more detail in Part 2 of this book.

Whatever the explanation may be, it appears there is a sympathetic nature within us to those events that occur in our world, as well as to others around us. We feel things that are about to happen for no definable reason, or we sense things that are happening to people we may know but who are far from us while they occur.

One of the most telling experiences I have had came my way when I was still in high school. To this day, it remains one of the most striking events that left no doubt we are able to perceive things in ways that are beyond our normal capabilities.

There was a junior schoolmate I had come to know by the time I was in grade 12. I think the other boy—I will call him Mike—was in the eleventh grade at the time. He also happened to be a member of the student council. Through some misguided belief that the student body would somehow welcome a jukebox in the lunchroom cafeteria, which played nothing but perpetual elevator music, Mike had managed to have the idea approved by the school faculty. Being somewhat outspoken in my opinions, both then and now, I voiced my disapproval of the genre of music to which the rest of us seemed forced to listen. I soon received the backing of every other student who typically occupied that area during their down time between classes.

After being appointed the spokesman for the little conflict we had all seemed to have created for ourselves, I asked for the music to either be changed or turned off altogether.

We all soon realized, however, that the majority of the students' pleas fell on deaf ears. Mike assured me that the school faculty unequivocally backed his rather displaced music selection, which seemed designed to pacify and numb us all into a state of mental paralysis. Soon a crowd gathered around both Mike and myself outside the cafeteria entrance, where I quickly commanded the audience. My points were heralded by the others present and though Mike loudly discounted my verbal condemnations, I still walked away from the debate as the clear winner.

Some time went by with the majority of the cafeteria crowd becoming more disgruntled with each passing day. Though the majority of the student body was clearly opposed to the forced jukebox music, Mike seemed to embody the same tyrannical mindset to which the school faculty clung. It did not matter what the popular opinion may have been—a few individuals had already chosen to impose a more serene atmosphere than the one to which we were accustomed. We all began to miss our previously enjoyed selections, coming by way of *The Rolling Stones*, *Led Zeppelin* and *Pink Floyd*.

Finally, I decided to take a page from the physics class and took the shortest route from point A to B. When we all finally hit our critical mass, I simply walked up to the jukebox and unplugged it. That fairly simple act, which required much less effort than anything I had done up to that point, resulted in a cacophony of hand-clapping and cheering.

Mike immediately got up and plugged the machine back in, which resulted in my encore performance.

At this point Mike marched up and began criticizing me in animated fashion. Some words were exchanged, wherein Mike finally pushed me into some chairs. A retaliation was offered, which immediately led to the entire altercation coming to an abrupt end and resulted in Mike storming off in a huff.

The faculty soon became involved, following this clearly anticipated boiling point reaching its apex. Once resolved, however, apologies were offered from both sides.

It is funny how heated disputes can often result in differing parties coming to appreciate each other with more respect than first exercised. It only took a little conflict to bring a better understanding of the underlying currents that caused it in the first place. Mike and I were soon friends and went on from there. We were quickly getting along better than we would have ever imagined during those dark and stormy days of what I like to call, 'The Jukebox War'.

(Incidentally, the classical rock we had come to love was soon returned as the default music selection.)

Following that incident, a number of months went by with events remaining rather dull and uneventful. Things remained mundane, that is, until I went to sleep one night before another school day was set to begin.

It was still the middle of the night when I apparently woke up in a car on the main road that went through a village directly to the south of where I lived. The car had burst into flame on that road as it headed into the village. As I sat there inside the burning vehicle I wondered, quite panicked, how it had all come to be. I was on the passenger side of the car and next to me, in the driver's seat, was Mike. He was screaming and crying out in agony. I tried to reach over and pull him out, but I could not seem to get a grip on him. The car continued to burn and soon the fire began to engulf my side just as it was consuming Mike. I could feel the flames hot and terribly painful as I tried to pull him free.

I woke up in a panic as a wave of relief washed over me. I quickly realized I was all right and that the whole thing had been nothing more than a bad dream. I looked at the clock beside my bed and realized it was still the middle of the night. Eventually I went back to sleep and woke up the next morning, stumbling out of bed and getting ready for another day of uncommitted learning.

With the dream from the night before still fresh in my mind, I noticed Mike did not seem to be in any of his usual classes. Most of the day had already gone by before one of my best friends approached and asked if I had heard the news.

He began to relate how Mike had been in a terrible car crash last night. He had apparently been driving toward the very village in my dream and had crashed head-on with another vehicle. Mike's car had erupted in fire and he had burned to death inside.

The news felt like a hammer hitting me between the eyes. A very *big* hammer!

By all accounts, the accident had occurred on that night right around the same time I had experienced the dream of

Mike burning inside the car.

It was uncanny. After hearing the mind-blowing news, I told my friend of the dream I had experienced.

Apart from the fact that this was a truly bizarre event which clearly meant something, I did go on to wonder why exactly I had experienced it. Though Mike and I had become friends by circumstance, I was certainly not as close to him as many of my other friends. The question remained, why I would I have witnessed his death after having known him for just a short time. There was nothing particularly remarkable about our relationship.

It was not actually until I began writing this book that it struck me perhaps the reason lay in something beyond our brief acquaintance. I began to wonder if we were souls who had known each other in a previous life. Maybe this was an old friend from a distant, past existence. It may be similar to encountering strangers in dreams who we sense we know far beyond this life.

After that event, many years would go before I would come to suspect I had astral traveled to the car on the night Mike had died. I had initially thought it to be a dream, but it was the most vivid dream I had ever had, to the point I was quite convinced it was completely real. What was most intriguing was that my consciousness seemed so strongly aware of what was happening during the accident that it was able to be at that very spot while the mayhem was occurring. This is part of the connection we seem to share and of which such old cultures as Australian Aborigines speak. It is a striking example of universal consciousness.

It seems there are encounters with people who suddenly appear in our lives at odd moments, but with whom we immediately have a connection that apparently defies reason. My belief is that we may have spent much of our lives with some beings in prior existences. Later, for whatever the reason, those same souls come back into our lives at crucial times, even if just momentarily, in order to teach us something important.

Considering the above examples, I have come to believe we are all bound to one another, whether aware of it or not. There are times when we appear to possess abilities most of us can not begin to fathom. The evolution of religion is just one cultural aspect that has been used to help make sense of, and explain, historical events which seem beyond understanding.

Cases have been recorded throughout history that describe unusual men and women who have had visions that seem so inexplicable they appear to be of a divine nature. Ezekiel and the wheel he saw in the sky is one example that lives centuries after its proclaimed occurrence. It has often been interpreted as a UFO encounter, long before such things as alien visitation became popular mythology.

As a youngster, I have been fascinated with UFOs (Unidentified Flying Objects), not so much for their currently believed ties to other worlds within the cosmos, but more for what they seem to represent throughout recorded history. Within our cultures, knowledge and technology have changed and the rationale for the existence of UFOs has, likewise, changed. In earlier times UFOs had been believed to be angels or beings from the heavens, far beyond our earthly understanding. Later, with the exploration of space and our expanded understanding of the universe, they have come to be regarded as messengers from the stars.

The argument has remained for a long time among respected scientists and theoretical physicists that UFOs could not possibly be from other planets circling distant stars. They account this declaration to the vast expanses and the related time which would be required to traverse them. Of course, we are basing that rationale on present technology and the laws of physics as we currently understand them. This is nothing to say of the new rules of physics that are currently challenging our traditional beliefs. Just as we seem to have the universe figured out, another discovery is made, which turns those preconceived notions upside down. Dark matter, quantum mechanics and string theory is currently leading cutting-edge minds in new directions. Even doorways to parallel universes existing on separate, extra-dimensional planes are being seriously considered, just as the Theory of Relativity is now accepted after years of initial doubt and reluctance.

I remember a particular morning, when I was quite young and returning from my morning hockey practice before lumbering off to school. I stood on the doorstep of my home and looked up at the sky.

Apparently out of nowhere, a disk shaped object came hurtling downwards, wobbling as it careened towards the ground behind the surrounding homes.

I was the only one outside at the time, so I could hardly blame anyone else for not believing what I had seen. Even after running to the back yard of a neighboring house where I was sure the object had crashed, I could find nothing. Everything was normal and as it should have been. Nevertheless, I remained stupefied by the experience.

TRANSFORMATION

Looking back on the event, it felt as though a doorway had opened up in the sky to show me something. I was seeing a vision, perhaps, that was not of my world. Something had simply allowed me to see it as I stood there wide awake, staring at things that seemed so completely real and, yet, seemed to defy reality. It may have been that the sight was real but it actually existed somewhere beyond my own physical plane. Perhaps I was seeing it in a completely different reality that my dulled mind was somehow able to sense.

More than anything these days, I look at such aberrations as UFOs and odd things in the sky as psychological manifestations that come from a place we have yet to understand, both in our own mind as well as within our understanding of what reality may truly be.

As a child, I did experience some strange events beyond those mentioned above.

On one occasion, a group of people who were taking care of me for the night decided they would like to visit a psychic healing club in the downtown core of the city. The two ringleaders dragged me along, as they were quite eager to witness the proceedings. It was the 1970s, after all; a time of exploration and discovery, so to speak.

Once we were there and immersed in this strange, paranormal subculture, it seemed we were watching a sort of magic show, without the dazzle of any actual tricks, mind you. With that in mind and given my young age at the time (I was about nine years old) I was probably the only one there who found the whole fiasco utterly boring. The participants—would-be 'patients'—seemed to be in a trance while so-called psychics hypnotically waved their hands over the bodies of their subjects. There were no puffs of smoke, or dramatic explosions, not even a pretty female assistant in a short, sequin outfit, and everything took place in relative quiet.

When it was all over and the lights came on, my caretakers for the night dragged me up to one of the psychics so they could have a more in depth discussion about what they had witnessed.

I later found out the couple who were taking care of me were hoping to be diagnosed as having some sort of psychic aura. Sadly for them, this was not to be.

The psychic disclosed that she saw no significant auras around either of my captors, but she did lean past them while gazing at me intently. The psychic revealed that she saw a vivid aura of a very unusual color; one she had never seen before. I do remember her saying that this aura was very significant and I should always remember what she told me. She explained that one day when I was older it could be very important.

It seems many people have their own explanations for life, along with a reason they might believe in an afterlife. So far, I have had several near death experiences but I have not heard any of the paramedics later tell me in confidence that they saw a beautiful aura around me as I was dying. Nor have I traveled off to a miraculous place of existence that dwells in a magical land. During the times my heart has stopped, everything has remained plain and dark. I do remember being consciously aware of still existing, mind you, even after becoming clinically dead.

For those who are believers in auras and what they may signify, I do not discount their meaning if they do exist. I simply have never seen one. I have seen other strange things but I am still waiting for the significance of this so-called aura, as seen by the psychic that day, to finally make an impression.

Through all of this there is one field of knowledge that helps to make sense of initially inexplicable events while keeping our own wandering imaginations somewhat grounded. This is the evolution of modern physics and what we know about it through hypothesis and mathematics, and then by way of scientific observation.

What is science, after all, but merely the natural laws of how the world around us behaves. These laws are observed after repeated examination that is always conducted under the same conditions with the same events and quantities applied a number of times so we are able to determine the outcome is not merely a random event.

Our minds were sufficiently warped by Einstein's theory of relativity, wherein he proved that space and time are directly linked to one another.

Generally stated, Einstein's findings were that as we travel through space, time is also affected, leading us to discover that the two are directly intertwined. More than sixty decades have passed as we have finally come to accept this fact, even though many of us may still not fully understand the finer workings of the concept.

More recently, quantum theory has challenged our traditional ideas of physics and has led us on a completely new path of understanding our universe; even our own existence. If there are still those individuals out there trying to grasp the theory of relativity, I feel for those who are attempting to understand the concepts of quantum mechanics.

What seems especially perplexing about quantum

theory is that much of it is based on probability. The rules governing this field of research seem to have more to do with the law of probabilities as applied to casinos and day-trading mentality than it does with hard science. Yet, it remains one of the most important fields of science to this day.

That one particular quantum particle must rotate 360 degrees not once, but twice, in order to come back to its original starting point seems difficult enough to grasp on its own. That a particle can exist in two or more different places at the same time seems equally bizarre. This surpasses the already established law that two objects can not occupy the same space at the same time. Now, they are saying that one object can occupy *two* spaces at the same time; even more.

As we become more knowledgeable in science, we seem to become more confounded by it. While we delve deeper into its mysteries, the laws seem to become more cryptic. Yet, it seems to be this apparent contradiction in science that makes consciousness all that more viable, especially when it comes to paranormal events. After all, if paranormal phenomenon is real, should there not exist some scientific law to explain it? It has always been that occurrences we witness in nature have been definable by science. During bygone ages, we have simply not understood the science well enough to explain it.

Today, however, groundbreaking researchers have been examining quantum mechanics, along with string theory, in order to explain and unravel such things as precognition and cosmic awareness. This could be a stretch, considering physicists are still not able to scientifically explain gravity (other than some theories).

TRANSFORMATION

More than any other field of science, quantum mechanics seems on the brink of validating the theory that the world around us only exists for as long as we are conscious of it. Such views of thinking would fall directly in line with one of the latest theories that the entire universe is nothing more than an image created by our awareness of it. Still, there is that question, from where did we come, along with all the information responsible for creating the world we know.

If we accept there is no end or beginning and that the universe has simply always existed, everything becomes more clear, along with life, death and perpetual existence. Within our ever changing world, our own existence is always taking on new meaning while constantly coming into question. A holographic universe would certainly support an infinite possibility. But could it really be that our world is nothing more than a projection which is being created for our own amusement? The mere thought that our existence in a 3-dimensional universe could be a creation of all our minds would certainly lend credence to the notion of clairvoyance. If our collective consciousness is actually creating the universe in which we live, it would make perfect sense that we would all be tied into one another.

With concepts of space-time and gravity being warped and bent by possibility, the notion of a beginning and end to time, itself, is becoming lost. Given discoveries in our understanding of quantum mechanics, it now looks as though time truly can exist in multiple instances. A moment in time can exist alongside a parallel moment, as well as many others, all presenting multiple possibilities at once while existing in different realities.

We have come to a point in our history where science and religion have begun to point in the same direction, rather than existing as a detriment and conflicting threat to each others' ideology. As science, religion and spiritualism seem to be converging, any astrologer would clearly state that now, even if just metaphorically, the stars have never been more aligned.

4

The Power of Knowing

Everyone, deep in their hearts, is waiting
for the end of the world to come.

- Haruki Murakami

Over the ages civilizations have faded, sometimes leaving little evidence behind from which the next great power might learn. It may be we simply were never destined to learn from our past. Instead, it could be more appropriate to begin the exercise all over, just to see what happens next time around. The world exists as a playground, into which we are sent in order to flirt with all possibility while hoping to discover something everlasting.

For as many times as we have been sent into this proving ground, we have never managed to devise the perfect formula, wherein we are all able to live harmoniously. It could be we were never meant to find perpetual contentment for as long as we are here. In the Buddhist tradition, perhaps we exist to simply learn from our suffering and failed potential. As long as physical existence is orchestrated to be imperfect, it is unlikely we will ever achieve true mastery over our environment, let alone ourselves.

From what the past has shown, this seems to be the case. None of us have truly evolved to the point we are able to put our own desires behind us. Human nature appears to be static. It remains the same throughout the eons we have purportedly existed. We never become greater beings, filled with a growing sense of humanitarianism. Instead, our basest nature continues to rule our every whim.

Any of us can witness this plainly enough by standing back and watching our cultural development flounder. History teaches this much through repeated examples. If we choose to delude ourselves into believing our existence on earth is becoming more decent, we are probably doomed to an infinite cycle of self-imposed futility. Evolution, in the intellectual sense, seems to be doing us no good. Great wonders are peppered throughout time, yet what do we have to show for it? If we have not grown compassionately in the last two or three hundred thousand years, maybe there is a reason.

It would be a much nicer alternative to think the world is not really meant for us and that it is merely a pit-stop on the way to something better. If spiritual growth can only come by way of physical suffering, this is precisely where we should be.

TRANSFORMATION

I was taught Christianity as a child, simply because this is what my family believed from generations before them. It was only appropriate I would be taught the same faith. Still, as much as the belief was impressed upon me, I was never able to embrace it. I always knew there was something beyond the world, based on what I had already seen during my emergence. Physical existence took those beliefs and did whatever it could in an attempt to change them. This was not because the cosmos had a higher design for me; it was simply because the people within my world wished me to change, just as they, themselves, had already changed.

Every participant in this life grapples with what they choose to embrace in order to survive their own, designed environment. It was not the cosmos, or the universe, or even the overwhelming consciousness of being, which struck out to alter my perception. It was every other person who had existed in the world before me. Those same people marched through life beside me while doing their best to alter my perspective and how I should view my reality. All those who had come into this life with a good head-start were the ones doing what they could to transform the world and my point of view into something with which they could deal.

No one was doing this consciously, mind you. It is nothing more than a spillover effect from the way all of us conform to a physical life in which we unintentionally influence everyone else with whom we come into contact. This is the blind divergence that alters both those around us as well as ourselves. Only after realizing I was being converted to move along with the herd mentality did I break from my imposed traditions and seek out alternate answers.

From the day of my birth I have always known we exist apart from this world. The inevitable always brought me back to the same point from where I had started. It does not matter how many people tell us reality is one way or another. As long as we feel it and know it, our knowledge of our existence keeps us on course.

This is the reason I say life is a test. Life defies our beliefs and pushes our limits. Death is also a test. When we fail at death we come back into life. As crazy as it may sound, there is a right way to die and a wrong way.

All of us know, deep down, that we have come from something else. We are born with it. The world tells us to stop believing what we already know. If we give in and become convinced that physical life is the only true existence, we become consumed and lose sight of ourselves. Only in death do we really get the chance to see this is not the case and are given an opportunity to change our way. If we do not realize this much in life, we can discover it somewhere beyond this brief existence.

I have always maintained a conviction that the knowledge of what we are and from where we come resides in every one of us.

From the moment of physical existence, even while traveling through life, I have felt something that has always been with me. It stirred with such intent, I could rarely deny it.

With every year of my childhood that passed, I sensed there was something about the world that was more than what we see. It may have been fleeting at first, but it eventually solidified into a cohesive thought. Soon, I felt it so unmistakably I would sometimes tell friends there was something coming our way that would shock and surprise every one of us.

When my parents moved from the city to the country, I would find myself riding to school on a bus, traveling through the countryside, back and forth. It was a far departure from my experience of growing up in the city. There, I could simply walk across a highway behind my house and soon be at school. I usually went with friends from the same neighborhood so we could talk on our short journey to the halls of education. The country bus ride was quite different, however. It gave me time to ponder and watch the serene hills and farm fields, which surrounded me, drift silently by.

Every once in a while I would get a glimmer of myself walking along the edge of some cornfield. The experience would often leave me feeling I had done that very thing before, but in another life. It was not until I was living in the country that the world became much more quiet and I gradually began to view things in a different way.

At first impatient and not at all happy with having left the city and my circle of friends, I fixed my mind on moving out of the house as soon as possible. I told some new classmates at school that I actually intended to move out that first year in order to find an apartment. I already had a part time job and felt I could go to work full time in order to make enough money to survive.

A classmate, with whom I had recently become close, actually talked me out of the idea and insisted I would be better off graduating first. I am glad I listened to him.

I resigned myself to the next four years of learning.

It seemed once I surrendered to the fact I was not going anywhere for several years, I began to view my world in a new light. I found myself actually listening to the natural landscape that surrounded me and, after just a little while, I began to hear what it was saying.

Resentful over having been plucked from my familiar existence within the urban sprawl and its associated mayhem—something off which I apparently fed throughout my formative years—I initially felt my new surroundings offered little opportunity. I have always been fairly resilient in adapting to my environment, however, and soon began to meld into the world of quiet that was all around me. In fact, I began to take journeys into the fields and forests at night, listening only to the sound of emptiness; something I would soon discover was not very empty at all.

I sat out there year after year, in a receptive state of meditation, listening to the world around me. Emptying my mind and allowing the influence of the universe to come flowing in, I soon began to see there was still something far beyond the physical. I opened up to the world. From that moment on, the world did the very same and opened up to me.

One of the most defining moments of my life (beyond my transformation into physical consciousness) took place after I had been living in the country for several years. Something occurred which had taken some time to finally awaken. The experience opened my eyes to the reality of human existence in a way it never had before.

It was during a day I would have normally been at school. On that occasion, the school faculty had declared a 'professional development day'—a self-imposed excuse for teachers to have some time for themselves under the guise of heightened educational insight. Thus, we all got to stay home.

I took the opportunity to spend the day out in the countryside communing with nature, as I had come to do on a routine basis. There was very little else to do for a youngster from the city back in those years. I had learned to adapt to a new kind of lifestyle far removed from what I had known before.

That day remains one of the most mystical of my life. It was on this particular occasion that I realized something truly profound after putting myself into a deep state of meditation.

What too few of us understand is that we exist in this world, but at the same time we do not. Part of us remains somewhere else. That part, which is beyond our physical existence, is still partially in the ether of forgotten reality. At times, it is close enough to touch. There are various ways to see it. One way is through lucid dreaming and astral projection. The fastest route is clearly through death. But we can also see it clearly through meditation. Once we have honed our mind to a state where it is similar to sleep while still being awake, we can realize the truth of ourselves and our existence.

It is one thing to pass from existence into life and to be confounded by such an experience. It is a fleeting moment that allows us to see how physical reality is dreamlike and hypnotic. It is another thing, entirely, to be in this world while at the same time seeing the reality beyond. Well, all I can say is that is something to truly be experienced. Only then does the clarity of many realities come washing over us.

At that point, everything I had always believed—that

the world does not actually exist the way we think—forced my eyes wide open. A deep sense of understanding everything—knowing what it meant all at once—washed over me. I knew in an instant that something remarkable had been revealed. For a moment that seemed to last forever, I saw reality as it exists beyond physical sight. It was so overwhelming that it immediately filled me with a euphoria unlike anything I had ever experienced.

Immediately following that, it began to rain. I ran deliriously up and down the road in front of my house howling at the sky in mad abandon. Yes, the neighbors likely thought I had gone insane, or had contracted rabies; both distinct possibilities where I lived. I was completely consumed by the knowledge that nothing in the world, or in our lives, was ever truly a question. There remained something hidden, not far behind what we come to accept as real. Physical reality was little more than a reflected glimpse.

I had been given a striking reminder that the world was not as obvious and simple as it seems on the surface. Life is a brief interlude that merely draws our attention away from one reality for the sake of another.

The years I had spent out in the fields and among the trees, meditating and communing, had apparently done something to the way my conscious mind perceived my environment. It is something I never spoke to anyone else about for many years, thereafter. The experience was quite similar to the one I had upon being born; knowing at once that I was between two worlds, each one a separate reality.

When I began doing research for this book, looking closely at the Eastern philosophies of the life, death and rebirth cycle, I found a number of them believe in carrying aspects of a previous life into the next one. This lent a fair amount of credence to what I had always felt was true for myself and for everyone else in the world. Hinduism, in particular, portends every soul that is not able to pass into the higher realms of existence, subsequently returning to this one, brings with it several retained memories from its prior existence.

As I stated at the beginning, it is quite possible we all enter the world knowing we just came from some place else. Like that dream we often have, it is still vivid the moment we come back to our waking reality. A few moments later, as we shower and get ready for the day, we soon realize the details are usually forgotten. We are still aware of having a dream; it is just that we no longer seem to remember the finer points of what it was about.

Every new life, which comes into the world, enters clean and uncorrupted (as far as the larger crowd is concerned).

This design works for a reason. Though every newborn child who enters the world may come into it with a degree of self-awareness, on most occasions we will never be privy to the potential prognostications we inadvertently bring. In our raw form, we exist in a state of before and after life. Tibetan Buddhists tell us we spend roughly 49 days wandering in a limbo between death and life as we choose the next existence upon which to embark. If we choose another physical incarnation (as many of us do), we come in with very little knowledge of anything before, free to learn it all again. Those of us who are focused and conscious enough to ascend to a higher existence move on, having learned from the failures and successes of our previous life. For those who doom themselves to repeat their stumble, they are simply not allowed to keep their memory as extra baggage while coming into the next life.

We simply can not know of our past failures in the physical world if that is what we have ordained for ourselves. The choice was ours to make in the first place, after all. Knowledge comes from self-realization. Remnants of the past merely hinder what we see and know in the here and now. We can not be encumbered by anything else that preceded us to this point if we are destined to find a higher awareness. Memories of another life would only stifle that learning process. So, we wander on, like travelers staggering through the trees, searching for a clear way until we find the path we missed during our last time around.

From my earlier experiences in communing with the universe, and the countryside that became my world, I learned each one of us has the power to quiet our mind and listen to what the cosmos is saying. We do not need to be religiously indoctrinated, but if we do follow a belief the mere awareness of our reality should not conflict with any single denomination. I have come to realize religions are all merely culturally diverse interpretations aimed at taking us to a common place that is inherent within all human beings, whether inert or otherwise.

All of us have that same thing inside. We are all spiritual beings and each has the power to feel that truth of consciousness, which is part of us.

It is because of this I soon realized life is not the preoccupation of getting to some final goal wherein we sit back and reflect fondly on our achievements once we are there. Existence is an evolving journey. We are not here to change the world either. Five thousand years of written history has enabled us to glean that for as long as people have been around there has always been conflict among us. The ruins at sites that are even older than the advent of writing leave us to conclude that many ancient civilizations ceased to exist due to conflict or natural, catastrophic events.

For many years I wanted to help change the way we all live and to make the world a better place—a prominent cliché. I realized later that one person can not change things for all people, nor do I think they are meant to. Life is a solitary journey. One person can, however, change another person's life, or make it somehow better. If we manage to affect just one other human being in a positive way, such an act can be just as important, if not even more rewarding.

Life, along with all its wonderful intricacies and unfortunate detriments, is meant to be experienced, not cured.

It seems on occasion so-called prophets and spiritual gurus have come to help guide us from our wandering and onto a path that eventually leads to some form of spiritual awakening. Often in pursuing that end, such people are mocked and scorned by a populace full of loathing.

In today's terms, if Jesus Christ were to walk the earth with his disciples, the world would likely look upon him and his happy band of 'do-gooders' with suspicion and contempt. In fact, throughout time redeemers have come, attempting to lead us toward hope and good will and away from our baser instincts. As witnessed in the past, these spiritual guides are usually persecuted by the predominant powers, as though fearful that such interlopers are here merely to disrupt the desirable environment that was so painstakingly established before them.

Human nature would indicate that the darker aspects of ourselves dictate our actions throughout existence. We have been this way for as long as modern humans have been around (at least 200,000 years; maybe even longer). So, why would we continue to be the way we are unless there were a grand design to it? If there were some greater meaning, would it not have presented itself by now?

It appears that moving into a higher existence takes great patience.

According to *The Tibetan Book of the Dead*, there are many worlds into which we can possibly enter, all of which are dependent upon our own developed state of self-awareness. In Buddhist philosophies, the world in which we presently find ourselves is among one of the lower realms into which one could possibly emerge. So, what does that tell us? Are we here to change the face of hell? Or are we here to serve time and learn from mistakes that may have possibly been repeated throughout ages we can not even imagine?

Hindus hold a similar belief to Buddhists, seeing our physical existence as just one of countless others. Realities and universes exist beyond time and are constantly being created; always evolving.

When we have actually reached a level worthy of our ideals, we will already be in that world where such efforts are deserving. Until then, it is time served.

This life is not just an experience; it is also a perpetual education that causes us to constantly change and re-examine our perception and beliefs. As we grow physically, it is in our interest to grow spiritually. Even for those who do not believe in an eternal soul, the spirit can also mean someone's mental evolution and the way they treat oneself, as well as those around them. Spiritual growth also accounts for how we fit into society and how we deal with common problems in life.

I have already suggested that many religions seem to be variations of the same theme. As far as feeling something inside that assures us there is a God, the notion might not be as esoteric as it sounds. Hindus believe every person's spirit is a piece of a Supreme Being which simply lives inside us. It is all part of a larger whole, in however a diminutive form.

Some Eastern philosophies believe it is the cosmic will of a universal consciousness to send some of us back into this mortal life while still being fully aware of the divine world that exists beyond. This is all for the purpose of helping to guide others onto an enriched path.

These divine beings of knowledge are apparently all around us. The Dalai Lama (spiritual leader of Tibet) is reputed to be an enlightened, perpetually conscious being who intentionally reincarnates in order to help the rest of us achieve transcendence.

Even in Western culture there are the Knights Templar, believed to be older than Christ himself. A secretive organization, it is sometimes speculated they guard a mystery to the meaning of life and the oldest customs of our people. I have known some members of this organization, which has evolved into the Freemasons, and there is something elegant in the proclamations they espouse today.

Never actively recruiting their members, a potential candidate must ask to be accepted into the organization. Even then, one must know someone who is already a member and who is willing to sponsor the likely inductee.

From what I am told, the bulk of Freemasons' ideology is to be the best human being they can, rich in moral fortitude and doing good will for their fellow humans. Whether this was always their doctrine or whether it is one that evolved through necessity, there is something that can be said for it. If the order were one that knew the true meaning of life, would it not be in keeping with many Eastern philosophies? Both essentially preach the enrichment of our souls through karma and becoming better people by doing good for others, rather than pursuing selfish ends.

Perhaps to this day the Knights Templar are sticking to a strict regimen of helping us all become better people, just like Buddhism, Hinduism, Christianity and a host of other religions.

As children, we seem to know more about honesty and simplicity than our parents, though we often lack the ability to articulate it. Eventually, we become like our parents anyway, taught constantly throughout our lives how to act, how to survive and how to lie (especially to ourselves).

When we come into the world, meanings seem clear and easily understood to us as children. There is no riddle and no mystery. It would make sense since children are much closer to the 'before life' than adults, who have had more time to drift further away. Those who have already been here for several decades are more susceptible to slip into oblivion as the world puts its hypnosis on them and fools them into believing this life is all there is.

Children are blessed because they are new to the physical world while still being quite close to the ethereal existence from where they just came. They are brand new and their souls are naked and untouched by the world from day one, privileged as they are able to stay that way for a while. Only upon interacting with the world over time do they start to change.

Anyone who can realize this in their formative years is fortunate because it gives them the power to shape their existence from the beginning. The same is true once we realize physical life is not what we think, but only a version of reality. Our existence here is simply another altered state of consciousness, but with the addition of a gross body.

If life actually is a sort of game, it is a peculiar one. I can sit quietly and meditate out on my country estate where the preoccupations of the world dissolve easily and I can know that the universe around us is forever pervasive. However, just like a lucid dream, if we become caught up in that world we manifest we soon forget where we are and eventually become enraptured. We can take time to dislocate ourselves from our present reality, but once that moment is given up the illusion takes over. Soon it is forgotten that we are sailing a ship on a sea and we become the sea upon which we sail. It is easy to become submersed and preoccupied with our physical predicament, forgetting it is nothing more than a passing thought. Instead, we begin to live inside a dream as though it is our only reality.

Considering this, it is easy to understand why the

Buddha had to devote so many years and self-sacrifice to his constant struggle. He had to remind himself that much of what existed in life was nothing more than illusion and temptation. The Buddha spent an extended period of time in meditation, attempting to separate the real from the illusive. Throughout that time, it is purported much of it was spent in spiritual battle, until he finally did reach enlightenment. For most of us, the world in which we exist seems so convincingly real by the time we are in adulthood that we become forever lost in it.

Eastern cultures, which have been around for thousands of years before ours, do believe in spiritual guides that come back in successive lives to reaffirm there is indeed an afterlife. They even bring back proof of their past lives in order to be confirmed as the next leader in taking their people to a higher level of awareness as reward for their focus. Every Dalai Lama of Tibet must pass a series of tests to prove they are reincarnated before leading the next generation of believers to a higher plane.

I have come to realize simple truths. I have wandered through this life while constantly experiencing challenges and conflict. Through most of those experiences the answers have come. Often, I have felt there is something that guides us through life, which seems ready to pull us out of a dilemma at exactly the moment we need it most.

When I was young there was a period of time during which I was picked on and beaten by bullies, and gangs of bullies, who permeated my neighborhood. After this went on for a while, I simply decided to fight back, contrary to my mother's insistence that I rise above it by not resorting to similar tactics. Surprisingly, I seemed to know how to sweep people to the ground, slip punches and dodge various attacks while at the same time counter-attacking my self-appointed antagonists.

Later, I developed a penchant for creative writing after having done practically no writing at all. I embarked on an education in science and theoretical physics, which also seemed to come out of nowhere, and I soon embraced concepts that my friends, colleagues and family felt were lost in an impalpable swamp.

It is as if I have lived many lives in the past and the experience from those previous excursions have remained deep inside me, even as I traveled from one existence into the next.

Life is constant struggle. The realization that it is more than just physical existence and that higher knowledge lies beyond our reality is the true awakening. It seems the problem with knowledge is that too few of us have a substantial amount of it. This could all be for good reason.

Many of us are lost in a fog of dim awareness. The journey of life may be easier for those within the developed part of our world, but that is simply because we have shut ourselves off to anything else. Our careers, family, and home is what we focus on throughout our lives. We do not question the reason for why we are here, other than it seems clear our goal is to work, raise children to follow in our footsteps and to plan for a retirement wherein we can relax for a few years, resting upon our accomplishments before we finally die.

For many of us, it has already been determined we will go through life with a singular purpose. That is not to suggest our efforts will be meaningless. Anyone who has, and will, follow the above blueprint will probably feel great joy at points in their life. They will also likely experience periods of despair, but that is merely part of the process. All of it is designed to encourage spiritual growth. Without it we would simply not be human.

In the very same way, we will often hang onto a belief there is something greater than ourselves, hoping there is a higher meaning that gives us purpose. Sometimes it will not easily be deciphered, but there will always be those who believe it to the point they are beyond even a fleeting moment of doubt.

Life is designed to be constructed around such uncertainty. Not only do we struggle with doubt, but also with misdirection and conflicting evidence. Everything around us is a clue and a test; a truth and a lie. We are handed a glimmer of hope and given as much reason to believe in a higher meaning, as well as having enough cause to doubt it all.

Why do many of us simply not know the truth while others claim to see it all without hindrance?

The answer could be fairly obvious for anyone who has seriously considered such aspects of life, death and eternal existence.

If we are meant to learn something in this life—if we are truly meant to accomplish something of substantive meaning—it could hardly come into being if we all knew the truth.

Imagine an entire populace placed on this earth, waiting to die, every single person knowing this is not their true life and that we come from some eternal existence where the minutia and idiocy of human nature and its many follies holds little meaning. If we all knew our physical lives were nothing but a brief sidebar in our never-ending existence and that none of it really accounts for anything, there would be no struggle. There would be no feelings of despair and no light of ambition to overcome obstacles in a strange land that seems out to get us. Without such challenge, we would simply sit back, tell ourselves that life is meaningless and give up until the time finally comes for us to die. Worse than that, there may even be those who would simply kill themselves, eager to get back to the more pure existence they had before coming here to the land of the living, as ironic as that may seem. Sadly enough, it is clear there are people and cults who already partake in such destructive rituals.

Our lives in the physical world would simply not work if we all knew the truth and retained the memories of our past existence. It is that very reason why most of us are simply not allowed to know the past, the future, or foreign realities that still await. It is our purpose to suffer in life and to struggle with it, as if this is the only life we will ever have. If not, the growth of our eternal spirit through such effort will simply fail to materialize.

Through all of this, there are still those who come into the world who know something more of our reality and more of our existence than others. Just as clearly as there is a reason that those of us are not allowed to know, there is also a rationale why those who *do* know, are in the minority. Those are the individuals who give us just enough to decide for ourselves.

The truly humble and sincere are not those self-described prophets who insist we must believe them and nothing else beyond what they say. Because there are also false prophets, our ability to believe in something beyond our understanding simply comes at the price of greater doubt. It gives us enough trepidation to remain dubious rather than embrace, without wavering, the veracity of those other spiritual gurus who may be true and just. Still, it leaves us open to interpret those beings as we might, some of us never sure, some skeptical and some eager to receive what is represented, simply because it illuminates something inside us. It could be laying dormant in that person's soul for all their life. Then, one day they see the world in a completely different way. It could even be as clear as a single act, or some globally reaching event that changes a huge portion of the population's view.

This is the power of knowing. Some things seem to us as abstract and surreal. Life may forever be that way until we die. Others will know. That knowledge will come about by way of a slowly, creeping glimmer that one day develops into a new kind of awakening. Or it may simply always be there, retreating and advancing back and forth in a mocking display that dares us to grab hold and go along for the ride.

5

Life As Illusion

the separation between past, present, and future,
is only an illusion, although a convincing one.

- Albert Einstein

Some things seem so real they challenge our idea of what
is and what is not. While doing research for this book, one
of the most thought provoking elements I came across was
that of dimethyltryptamine (DMT). This is a chemical that
exists in all of us, as well as numerous other animals and
many plant species. It appears to be the most abundant,
natural psychedelic substance in existence, as well as the
strongest. Our body produces it as a natural part of our
metabolic process, yet we are still not sure why.

Even though this chemical is thought by some to be a
natural secretion of our active brain, its cultivation beyond

that means is largely frowned upon by Western authorities. However, people have been known to ingest the drug for various reasons. Experiences have been described as life altering, to the point that users no longer look at their own world the same way as they did before using DMT.

The following points are derived from articles and interviews put out by DMT researchers, as well as from studies that were conducted by Dr. Rick Strassman among test subjects and detailed in his book, *DMT: The Spirit Molecule*. At the very least, those experiences have been some of the most bizarre on record, as well as being intuitively disturbing:

In its recreational form, the drug is often smoked. By accounts, only two or three inhalations are required to send the user to what might be described as 'the other side'. With one or two puffs of the substance, reality becomes much sharper, colors more striking and music becomes emotionally intense. The third puff usually results in the user breaking through a membrane that separates our reality from something else. A crackling sound like bursting bubble-wrap is usually described, wherein the user penetrates the membrane and finds oneself in another world, or another reality altogether. At once, beings that are round in shape come rushing to meet the DMT user. They seem elf-like and speak excitedly, saying things like, "You made it, you made it!" and "You're here! We're so glad! We've been waiting!"

All the detail about the world the user encounters is said to be indescribable, according to those who have had the experience. They talk of the round, elf-like beings as becoming intensely overjoyed while projecting overwhelming feelings of love and connectedness to those who cross over. Users inexplicably experience a great love and connectedness toward the beings also, but are unsure why. While the world is striking and emotionally consuming, many users describe the round beings as often having no depth, as though they are actually 2-dimensional. Whether this has anything to do with the holographic universe theory is difficult to say, but immediately the implication becomes provocative.

That many users appear to go to this same place is also quite perplexing.

The experiences that are had by users of DMT are not prolonged, but they do end up being very overpowering during the brief journey; no longer than half an hour in duration, by most accounts.

Upon learning of DMT, I had to wonder if this could be a facilitator, of some sort, that tears down what separates one reality from another. Even after the first or second puff, users sometimes see this other world while still being aware of their own reality.

Though the chemical is not nearly as well known as LSD or mescaline, DMT has long been extracted from local plants in South America where indigenous tribes commonly ingest it, especially during rituals. Its affect is still not fully understood by those within the major region of the North American continent. Still, it offers enticing possibilities concerning the afterlife—some doctors link it to near death experiences—and the world that exists beyond our physical perception.

By some accounts, life is thought to be a type of mirage that our consciousness merely perceives as reality. Could it be all the stirrings we feel are nothing less than the imbedded memories of an eternal awareness? For as long as we exist here, letting go of such notions as prior lives sometimes becomes preferable in order for our present reality to make sense. Throughout the millenia some ancient philosophies have been suggesting physical existence is illusory, we may now be at a point where we can scientifically prove the illusion is real (as contradictory as that may sound!).

The promulgation of relativity, quantum mechanics and string theory have emerged to reveal our existence and our universe as something that possibly manifests due to our own conscious awareness. With these very sciences, it has come to a point where we can actually consider that all we see around us may be a creation of our own mind. It sounds very fanciful, I know, but if you bear with me for a few more pages I will do my best to explain the concept behind it.

As we have seen, theories in physics over the past several decades have shown a way of proving themselves and becoming real, as far as we understand them, that is.

One of the most fascinating fields of study that lends credence to our concept of reality is the world of quantum mechanics. Just like classical physics (established by such notables as Sir Isaac Newton, Galileo Galilei and Nicolaus Copernicus) enabled us to define our world and make sense of how it works, modern physics builds upon that foundation by digging further below the layers of physical laws that have validated our universe for centuries. In comparison to classical physics, realizations such as quantum mechanics is fairly new, in the same way Albert Einstein's scientific breakthrough in his Special Theory of

Relativity is a fairly new development of modern physics.

It has been a theory and a philosophical pondering throughout our history that life is not as steady and static a phenomenon as many of us have come to believe. All quantum mechanics has done, of late, is lend quantifiable evidence to the argument that certain things around us may exist simply because *we* exist.

It is an audacious view to take, granted, but throughout our lives there has been a persistent sense that there must be something to this theory. Homo sapiens have existed for about 200,000 years, by archeological account. There is also the 6 million years our ancestors are estimated to have existed before then. During our more recent recordings of human history, however, there has always been that notion of the true meaning of our place on earth and how it has come about.

I have spent a fair deal of time contemplating these things, mostly because I have seen there is an existence before we spring to life in the physical world. Because of this, there must logically be something beyond what we see while we are here. How we define it is usually dependent on our upbringing and evolving education.

I have been put on a religious path due to my family's tradition of Christianity. I have also gone through the anthropological journey, to discover there was something eventually missing from that explanation as well. While still a young boy I began to study theoretical physics through my school years and for many years afterward. I do not believe I realized it at the time, but the study of science was gradually guiding me toward yet another possible explanation for our existence.

In the end, I have found all these schools of thought

and various studies appear to converge with one another, rendering variations on the same theme. It has evolved that the Catholic Church now believes science is not the witchcraft it was once thought and is simply a valid means of explaining our natural world. The Vatican currently has their own astronomical observatory, contrary to a couple thousand years ago when such pursuits were considered heresy.

What I found particularly interesting during my pursuit of the reason for human existence is that it has only been in the past six or seven years I have begun to see that quantum mechanics may be able to explain something we have been asking ourselves for eons.

One of the most befuddling interpretations of quantum mechanics is the notion that something does not exist unless there is an actual observer to verify it exists (at least in some form). This is speaking on a subatomic level, mind you, but some physicists argue it can be applied to a macro level as well. However, I am sure there would be a valid argument that if all people were suddenly vaporized, the trees and the roads and the planet on which we lived would still be there.

Then again, maybe not! This is how bizarre science is becoming.

It is the theory of relativity and black hole physics, along with quantum mechanics and the relatively new development of string theory, that align with each other and point us toward the next realization. Scientific theories are presently attempting to validate one another and lend credence to the theory that the universe does not exist in the way we have always taken for granted.

My greatest questions have always been, "how could

the universe have never existed and then suddenly it did?" and "how could we have never existed before the moment of our birth and will cease to exist upon death?"

These two fundamental questions seem to be deeply rooted in each other. Yet, declaring there is a beginning and end to both seems completely self-defeating.

As I grew and was educated that we will eventually all die, simply to no longer exist, my greatest argument has always centered around awareness. I could never get past the possibility that we would simply no longer consciously perpetuate. One of my rationales was that all of us are a form of energy. As best as I can describe it, consciousness may also be a type of energy. It seems inconceivable that conscious awareness could suddenly cease to exist, whether in one form or another. Science has proved that energy can never truly be destroyed and that it simply transforms; something which is known as the law of conservation within the field of thermodynamics.

Astrophysicists suggest that the universe will one day collapse in on itself and there will no longer be an existence for anything or anyone. To this day the Big Bang is the most scientifically accepted explanation for how our existence came into being. At some point there was nothing—there was no universe, there was no space or time and there was no conscious awareness. Then everything came to exist in a massive explosion. Within an instant, space-time is believed to have expanded faster than the speed of light!

It all goes back to our place here in this very brief life we have on earth. Our physical comprehension is finite and we feel there must be a logical sequence of events in order to understand its reason. Thoughts of infinity just do not seem to sit well with us. Yet, we have proved infinity does exist, even if only on paper. Mathematical formulas, after all, remain the cornerstone of science. Many physical laws that have been established were first proved on paper before becoming accepted fact.

I am also a bit of a holdout from the more contemporary notions. I have an easier time believing in infinity than I do in a beginning and an end. When first entering this world, I felt that infinity was everything. Years later, I was informed there could be no such thing. I grappled with what I was being taught and found great conflict in the type of education most of us receive. For the longest time, I did not believe in death. To me, death was only going back to where I was before being born. Nothing ever ended. During most of my younger years, life seemed more like a dream than what we accept as true reality. Time goes by and it becomes difficult to differentiate between one dream and another and what is real from one waking moment to the next. But, then, all concepts of reality appear to be entirely subjective.

What quantum mechanics does for us now is offer a deeper insight into how the world and existence may actually work. Of course, we said the same thing when we discovered the atom. Experimentation has shown there are certain particles, or quantum objects, that often exist in one form or another for as long as we are there to observe them. Perhaps it is merely our conscious state that is creating these quantum sized particles for our benefit. Still, other particles have been noted to exist simultaneously, the same object existing in several different positions at once.

Such odd behavior could help validate the notion of

higher dimensions; dimensions we have theorized but do not yet completely understand. That some of these particles which underlie our known universe only exist because we are here to consciously manifest them would also lend some support to our universe existing as a result of our conscious projection. That none of us may actually be here and that we are conjuring our entire existence and the universe around us from some, as yet, unknown point of origin could be explained by quantum theory.

Then again, maybe we are not projecting our reality from a set point but are actually creating it all around us while being part of it.

All this may sound completely nonsensical. That our existence within the universe we have come to love and know may be nothing more than a hallucination would be a great insult to many people. But science has presented this as an actual plausibility through both quantum mechanics and string theory. This is what has become known as the Holographic Universe Theory and some very well known and respected physicists around the world have already been supporting it as a real possibility.

Essentially, the theory proposes we are not living in a 3-dimensional world as we know it. The holographic universe actually suggests we exist in a 2-dimensional reality and that we are being projected into a 3-dimensional existence. That we may actually exist as beings in only two dimensions seems peculiar, to say the least. If anything, should we not be projecting ourselves into an equal form of reality? How could we possibly understand something that would seem beyond understanding to a 2-dimensional form of life?

In essence, however, we already do the same thing

every time we dream. We suppose we exist in a 3-dimensional world, but during sleep we project ourselves into a dreamworld where the normal laws of our waking reality no longer apply. Instead, we can ascend to do things that would be physically impossible while awake. Our dreams would seem as limitless as projecting ourselves from a 2-dimensional world into a 3-dimensional reality. If the holographic universe proves to be real, then our waking reality might truly be just another type of dream; an illusion indistinguishable from any other.

The author of *Row, Row, Row Your Boat*, Eliphalet Oram Lyte, may have known something long before current theoretical physicists ever had an inkling. The familiar nursery rhyme was published in the year, 1881, long before modern physics came into being.

How exactly does this holographic universe theory work, you may wonder. While it is simple to understand the end result, how we arrive at that end is a bit more complicated.

Essentially, the theory states that any 3-dimensional form can be encoded on a 2-dimensional space. String theory describes a lower dimensional existence of 3-dimensional space, wherein all information is stored on a 2-dimensional surface in the same way a black hole stores information on its surface. Once something has fallen past the event horizon of a black hole (the point from which escape from its gravitational pull is impossible), that information becomes trapped. This is quite like the information stored in a hologram on a credit card. Black hole physics is largely responsible for lending substantive equations to prove the holographic theory to be possible. This is not to say we may all be living inside a black hole, but this is the science that supports the theory.

Oddly enough, science points out we do not really need a third dimension in order to exist. Furthermore, there is evidence that our universe contains less information than required by its three dimensional interpretation. Experimentation has shown that when we get close enough to the fabric of the universe, its definition becomes blurry, like that of a hologram. Professor Leonard Susskind, a physics professor at Stanford University, posited that because the universe is surrounded by a horizon in time, the information that creates the 3-dimensional universe may be contained there. Still, other physicists, such as Professor Jacob Bekenstein, believe the source may lie somewhere else.

The thought that our physical reality may be a manifestation of our conscious projection should be a rather empowering prospect.

Every time I have had a brush with death, I have felt very little fear. Quite to the contrary, I have usually felt a strange comfort. The realization that death is not a bad thing and that we do not ever truly die is a greatly liberating sensation. It allows us to go through life with a positive attitude. Like a lucid dream, we become fully aware of our reality and are free to manipulate it as we see fit. If the entire population of our planet were like this we would all be much more complacent and accepting of our fellow man and woman. Ill-will toward one another would vanish. Conflict would dissolve and we would embrace each other for who we are, realizing every one of us is just a reflection of ourselves, in whatever shape or form.

Given that   life would become so much easier to

understand, why do we not all have this insight? Clearly, as thousands of years have shown, we do not become more wise and compassionate over time. War and prejudicial disposition follow us throughout our existence. If there is one positive takeaway from this it is that our conflicted nature does make history a more colorful read.

Despite such shortcomings, the phenomenon of life in this world is not without purpose. We may possibly come into the world on a completely voluntary basis, though we are likely not aware of it. Many philosophies suggest we come into a physical reality due to our flawed nature. According to Buddhists, however, that flaw is largely self-imposed, though quite likely on a subconscious level as it is completely forgotten by the time we are here.

Time as Illusion

Throughout our world we have great minds which can hardly be grasped at times, even after seeing proof of their brilliance. I have often touted theoretical physicists as modern day Buddhas for the simple reason they seem to understand concepts and states of reality many of us can not fathom. Those who were far ahead of their time, such as Albert Einstein, Nikola Tesla and Stephen Hawking, came up with their breakthroughs by first pondering a problem for which there seemed no immediate answer. Once something made sense in their mind, they applied mathematics in order to prove whether or not their perceived solution could possibly be real.

If one person can simply think about something, imagine it to be real, and then be able to prove it in the physical world, there is a reason for that. It is this ability which suggests we contain knowledge of which we are not always aware, but resides in all of us. Some people are simply closer to that knowledge than others.

As past centuries have shown, anything that was initially imagined has eventually been created, or discovered. We imagined flight, space travel, the atom, the horseless carriage, along with countless other concepts that were far flung and, at the time, ridiculed as absolute nonsense. Yet, through perseverance and determination we have made all those previously nonsensical flights of fancy a reality. And it seems we will continue to do so.

Just like our dreamworld, as long as we are aware we can manipulate our environment and realize it as a world that can be influenced by our will, whatever was once imagination eventually becomes real. Perhaps it was even created before we imagined it.

In the same way some theoretical physicists seem to have a looking glass into the finer workings of our world, some of us are able to sense things that are about to happen perhaps simply because they already *have* happened.

Time and space are strange notions, as we have learned. Time, itself, is largely an invention of our own design in order to measure one moment to the next. It is a contrived idea that makes sense of every second we live and breathe throughout our life. If we did not impose such stilted restrictions upon our present reality, time may simply not exist; at least not in the way we currently know.

Those of us who see things happening in the future may simply be more tuned into the universe and what is occurring all around us. This is why some people claim to have the ability to forecast the future. They are able to do so because they are not really forecasting the future at all. Those clairvoyant types may be doing nothing more than describing a moment that already exists but which lies somewhere beyond the current view most of us have the ability to see.

Einstein's revelation, described by his Special Theory of Relativity, defines time as being a way to explain the fabric of 3-dimensional space from a certain perspective. Since space is always present, time may also exist all at once, including past and future. Essentially, because time is part of space, the past and the future could likewise exist within it at all moments. Past and future would actually be just another way to interpret what we really consider as each moment that is 'now'.

(See Appendix, A New Model of Time, for more on this).

Looking at this on a quantum level, it could be said that the future is just a point in space where we currently do not happen to be. We may be at that point eventually, but for now we exist at another point, even though the point we call the future also exists simultaneously, but beyond our view. It is simply further away from us while residing in the same space. If we consider quantum entanglement, where what happens to a particle at one point in space can simultaneously affect another particle in the same way while existing miles apart, it may be possible to use this analogy to explain precognition. The particle that is miles away is the future, while the other particle that is entangled is actually us, still in the present. Both the present and future exist at the same time since they are a construct of space. Through entanglement there is a direct channel that enables us to commune with the future, or at least sense it without seeing it.

Quantum physicists would probably roll their eyes at this analogy. Then again, if time were actually a static medium existing within space itself, it would stretch across all distance and we would be able to travel back and forth at our leisure, just as we do across space. This would mean each static direction drawn through space and time would contain all moments, past, present and future. For the most part, those moments simply remain hidden from us while we exist within a physical reality. That would make sense. If we were to become unstuck from time, we would exist in the past and future at the same moment that is now. A higher existence beyond our present understanding may very well be suited to such a scenario, but this would be an extremely confusing way for us to live within a physical reality. We are spared such an ordeal by engineering finite concepts of time that hide such other possibilities from our interpretive brain.

Perhaps it is conscious perception that enables us to sense other moments in time, while keeping us from wandering too far from the present.

I can count back to numerous incidents, personally, where strange phenomenon of forecasting future events have occurred that seem to defy logic. When the present catches up to the future it is like joining two ends of a line to form a circle.

If physical existence is nothing but a projection, like a movie screen that depicts many singular moments, perhaps there is much more that, for now, remains hidden behind the projector.

6

Ancient Cultures and Lost Civilizations

Humans and Gods

For as long as we know the human race has existed, our belief in a higher power has also existed.

In our fast-paced, technologically advancing world, religion actually appears to be on a decline. That is, it seems to be losing popularity here in the West, as well as some other pockets of the world. In most areas of the globe, however, religion and spirituality remains in abundance.

It is of particular interest that the oldest living culture we know, Australian Aborigines, maintain an unflinching belief in higher powers of existence. What is worthy of note is that the Aborigine culture of Australia is purportedly 50,000 years old, while some anthropologists argue it is closer to having existed for 65,000 years. In all that time, the Aborigines' conviction in spiritualism and worlds that exist beyond our own has never faltered.

There have been many passing eons and evolutions of religion. Yet, even with those years of adherence over the acceptance of higher realities to our existence, the very basis of spirituality has really not deviated. It remains steadfast, even as culture, intellect and technology ride the ebb and flow of human development.

The oldest religion that has existed during man's presence on earth is actually not even technically a religion. It is more aptly described as a belief system, or even a way of life. According to historical records and actual, physical evidence, it can be traced back to Africa, 70,000 years ago. To this day, it is also practiced by many cultures in Asia and North America. However, since this belief system has been thought to be part of many ancient cultures since the development of the modern, human brain, anthropologists believe it may be as old as 200,000 years. Some argue it could even be closer to 300,000 years.

Whatever the difference may be, both estimates are still quite old. It also makes this philosophy the oldest of beliefs in the history of human beings.

This is essentially what the native North American people held, who lived here 10,000 to 12,000 years before being invaded by Europeans. The term for it is 'animism' (or more scientifically, Primal-Indigenous), which comes from the Latin word, 'anima', which means breath, or inner self, or soul. The word animism was apparently coined in 1871 by British anthropologist, Sir Edward Burnett Tylor. It is actually estimated that 40 percent of the earth's population practice some form of animism to this day, including a portion of Christians, as odd as that may seem given its pagan connotations.

Essentially, animism is the belief that a soul, or spirit, inhabits every living thing on earth. Going even further than that, it maintains that spirit also inhabits inanimate objects, such as rocks and water. Even the heavens, the stars and the planets possess this spirit energy. There is belief in a god, or Supreme Being, but there is also the belief in lesser gods, who sometimes interact with the physical world. Since animism has been around, every other religion that has been invented has some underlying theme that has been derived from the very same principles of animism.

Because animism came into existence long before writing was invented, no written texts exist to describe its origin. Instead, it is passed down from one generation to the next in the form of spoken stories that teach each new crop of youngsters the belief system. This follows similar traditions to those of native North American tribes, such as the Navajo of the USA's Southwest.

Looking at animism from an objective point, it does hold many parallels to science and modern physics. After all, everything in the world, animate and inanimate, is made up of molecules and atoms, as are the stars and heavenly bodies. These molecules are constantly moving, whether we actually see it or not, and are a form of energy. Those scientists who define any notion of a soul, or spirit, can best equate it to a form of energy. Since energy can never actually be destroyed, it is an interesting analogy for eternal life.

Though it is estimated that a little under half the world's people practice some form of animism, empirically speaking for the sake of statistics, it is judged that about 300 million people actively practice it as their sole religion. Much of the split between those figures depends on how animism is truly defined. Still, it is one of the world's most widely followed philosophies and is most clearly its oldest.

The world's second oldest religion is Hinduism. It is estimated as being between 3,500 years and 4,500 years old, depending again on one's interpretation of its true origin. Even though it is one of the older philosophies, it is also the world's 4th most widely practiced religion, having roughly 900 million followers as of this writing.

It sometimes seems somewhat ironic that the world's two most popular religions—something we will get to shortly—are also among the younger religions on the linear time scale of history.

The religion of Islam is the 2nd most practiced religion, with about 1.3 billion followers to date. It is one of the youngest religions, being only 1,400 years old, with the religion of Shinto being just a little younger and Sikhism being roughly 500 years old.

Many people would probably not be surprised to find that Christianity is the most practiced religion today, statistically speaking of course. I have asked some people, tongue in cheek, if they know how old Christianity actually is. Surprisingly, many have been dumbfounded by the question, some actually guessing 4,000 to 5,000 years old (some of these people were in their 50s, as incredible as that may sound). Since I am writing this part of the book in the year 2017, I think we can accurately say how old Christianity really is, given any particular year. It does, however, point to a significant demographic that has lost touch with their spiritual upbringing.

Despite that, as I write these words Christianity has about 2.1 billion followers.

Since Christianity is much younger than many of the other popular religions, some might wonder how it came to be the most widely practiced religion in the world.

I qualify this by looking back at historical records, during a time when the Catholic church was sending out emissaries to practically every corner of the world. They set up missions in South America, Africa and the Middle East, as well as parts of the world where so-called 'savages' had never before seen a European. Many of these missionaries were butchered by the native people who were, literally, dead set against being converted by what they usually viewed as an invasion of their idyllic and remote lifestyle. The missionaries were undaunted, however, and over the centuries large portions of the so-called 'dark territories' were converted to what became known as civilized people. This, of course, came about following their eventual submission and embrace of the Christian God, even if it killed a lot of them in doing so.

To this day, I believe the Christian faith is so popular for the simple reason it does not accept reincarnation as a natural manifestation of the cycle of life and death. I suppose it may be easier and more placating to view one's life as a brief moment in the physical world, after which we all ascend to heaven. That is unless, of course, we have committed extremely heinous acts for which the Christian God sees fit to punish. As long as we live a good Christian life, we can die as contented beings never having to worry about coming into this world again.

In the West, we have so embraced technology and

materialism that it has become easier to dismiss notions of God, a Supreme Being and the afterlife in favor of defining ourselves as disciples of pure science. It seems the most recent religions, from Christianity to Islam, are more focused on one life and one existence, never having to repeat the pain of birth beyond a single, terrifying moment.

Contrasting the examples above, the latest evolution in religion appears to be that of an 'anti-religion'. This is the belief that no higher power exists beyond the material world of what can be seen and touched. In reality, one could say the third largest demographic of religious sects are secular, non-conformists and disbelievers. They are adamant there is no God—one could almost say they are actually religious about *not* being religious—and that we are here simply to live and die, never to be heard from again. In the end we all turn to dust and each one of our lives eventually becomes meaningless; forgotten once our genealogical bloodline runs dry.

Looking at animism, it is interesting that the next oldest religion, Hinduism, draws many parallels from the oldest of religions. Both philosophies believe in a Supreme Being while also believing in many lesser gods. The two also embrace the notion of many worlds, or planes of existence, beyond our physical life, which some contend we move between. Belief in an eternal spirit is also integral to both philosophies.

Elements of Hinduism are found in the next two most widely practiced religions, those being Chinese Traditional and Buddhism, in that order.

Chinese Traditional is a mix of Chinese folk religion, Confucianism, Buddhism and Taoism. The last three are separate religions, which means the Chinese are open to many aspects of all four. There is no central headquarters for the philosophy and no founding individual. Many practice an interaction of all the faiths and, as of this writing, roughly 394 million people take part in the religion. It is generally accepted that Chinese Traditional philosophy is at least 3,600 years old, though some estimate it as being more than 7,000 years old. Whatever the real number may be, it must certainly have evolved over time, considering Buddhism was not actually founded until about 2,500 years ago.

As for Buddhists, their numbers are roughly 376 million, which puts them almost on equal footing with Chinese Traditional practitioners.

Anyone who has studied or practiced Buddhism should realize that though there is a belief in the notion of reincarnation, it does not support the idea of an eternal spirit in each one of us in the same way Hindus believe in the spirit. Buddhism advocates the soul's ego becoming lost following each death, though the consciousness remains. In this way the spirit is able to come back continually, sometimes thousands, or even 100,000 times, before becoming enlightened enough to reach Nirvana. Buddhism does suggest there are many realities beyond this one. According to their scriptures, there are four sub-human realms of existence—some of them could be equated to a type of hell—and twenty-six higher realms above our own. There is only one 'human' realm, which happens to be the one we presently inhabit.

This contrasts markedly with the older religion of Hinduism, which holds there is a vastly greater number of realms than what Buddhists have come to believe. In fact, Hindus believe those realms are without limit and are constantly being created, according to Bhagavata Purana texts. (There are also the 14 Lokas of Hindu mythology, though these are thought by some to be various levels of conscious awareness). While Hinduism supports the belief in infinite worlds, it also holds that creation is a dynamic reality that never stops.

I should take a moment to point out there is a very devoutly followed religion I have not included above. This is simply because the numbers are nowhere near that of the more popular religions already mentioned. When I tell you which one it is you will clearly know why. As you may have already guessed, that religion is Judaism.

The most followed religions, from the ones that have been around a long time to the ones that are fairly new, bear a striking contrast which I think requires some clarity. Whereas almost every religion essentially indicates a Supreme Being exists and that the soul is constant, it seems only the two most popular faiths are also among the youngest while, simultaneously, diverging from the older religions. Though Hinduism, Buddhism, Chinese Traditional and Primal-Indigenous (animism) have been around considerably longer, it appears the more recent religions of Christianity and Islam are responsible for the greatest conflicts with which we are currently faced. Many have been slaughtered in the name of Christianity and Islam. Yet, the older religions do not advocate the conversion of others to their own faith, nor do they promote the idea of murderous or suicidal tendencies, which are brought on by more radical and extreme divisions.

Christianity and Islam have both had extreme sects which may be partially responsible for that percentage of the population turning their back on religion and embracing atheism. From a nonreligious, technocratic perspective, it must surely seem the more dominant options of religious following are the most conflicted.

Considering animism has clearly been around longer than any other philosophy, it appears to be a faith that grew out of a peoples' simple ability to sense their surrounding on a purely intuitive level. This came long before more formal and institutional religions sprang into existence. There was no noise coming from splintered cultures and civilizations, telling the many indigenous tribes what they should believe. Those ancient peoples had already figured that out on their own, long before modern civilizations. Animists saw the world around them in its most naked form and felt a deep connection to it; a connection so deep as to truly respect the world and everything it offered them. In keeping with such a humble edict, its followers only took enough from the land in order to sustain themselves. Such a belief may be the most spiritual of all religions. Merely because those people were not as socially, culturally or technologically advanced as later civilizations, does not diminish their spiritual depth. Actually, they may have been *more* culturally advanced than us. After all, they did not live in a world of constant conflict and perpetual greed, spurred on by religious fanaticism that seemed bent on destroying their own development every few thousand years or so.

Considering these aspects, it may even be ironic that Christians view such 'pagan' pursuits as being without a belief in a god. In fact, the very opposite is true. It is the earliest belief in spirituality and one that accepts the natural world for what it is rather than trying to change it to fit into its own, contrived model.

So what of the third largest demographic to which I briefly alluded above?

At this writing, there are approximately 1.1 billion nonreligious followers. Given that as of August, 2016, there are judged to be about 7.4 billion people occupying the world, this would seem a fairly significant number. What is more significant is that nonreligious members of the population have been growing as the world modernizes —mainly the industrialized West—and it appears they will continue to grow. It is judged that a quarter of the population in the USA is now nonreligious.

That religion appears to be dying in the modernized West would make some sense as people embrace science and technology above all else. It is far easier to believe in that which is purely physically than in something that has rarely been seen by some, or never seen by others. For those atheists and agnostics, the worship of a higher power becomes that of machine and pharmaceuticals. It is not surprising that nonreligious peoples have grown primarily in North America, Europe, Australia and New Zealand, where the development of technology and science is most prevalent. With the rise of communism in China there are also growing numbers of nonreligious people in that region, while former communist countries have seen their religious numbers actually begin to grow.

Studies have linked the steady rise in crime and conflict to the rise in nonreligious followers. It would make a degree of sense that if growing numbers of people believe death is the ultimate end and there is no Supreme Being to judge them for their actions, some would feel free to kill, rape, steal and otherwise plunder without fear of consequence, other than from their fellow man. The loss of religion seems to accompany the loss of humanity, as if spirituality is tightly connected to our human, moral fiber.

It should be pointed out, however, that even given these statistics it is becoming more evident that a portion of those secular members believe there is still a form of existence after death. This peculiar aspect would seem to go against the grain of being dismissive of higher powers and spiritual continuity. When considering what this means, it could simply point to a belief in spirituality that is devoid of organized religious overtures. Either that or some such individuals still wish to believe they will continue after death, no matter what may be their faith, or lack thereof. The desperation of survival is a powerful force, after all.

Ruins and Relics

The remains of past civilizations are strewn across the face of the globe and throughout the annals of history. Ancient ruins dot our planet's aging landscape like pieces of a puzzle waiting to be reassembled. If those pieces were simply primitive building stones that our ancestors used to construct their cities, we would be content in that knowledge and would walk through our present lives knowing we are the descendants that shine beyond them in our mastery of the world around us.

The truth is, however, those ancestors seem to have attained certain knowledge during a time we could not have imagined such scientific insights rivaling that of our present. Perhaps this is wherein the folly of our ways lie.

Who is to say we are more advanced now than we once were?

It seems logical to believe that history and the footprints of our forefathers would have followed a linear, cohesive line which we could easily retrace. Yet, there appear to be vast gaps in our history from one culture and time to another. This leaves us with incomplete records of those who came before. The best we can do is piece together remnants without understanding some of those eons from one delineated leap to another.

Such cultures as the Maya, Inca, Ancient Greece and Egypt, seem to defy our understanding. Those long lost civilizations appear to have possessed knowledge we are still attempting to grasp today. In fact, there have been many cultures that appear to have possessed technology and understanding that defy what we believe they could have possessed during their time. It is incredible, actually, to think how this could be.

It is also quite remarkable how there have been ancient cultures that have thrived for thousands of years without ever having the need to evolve in a technological way, as we have in the West. Native North Americans thrived and lived harmoniously for thousands of years before Europeans threw that balance into disarray.

What of the natural forces of the earth that past civilizations were able to harness? If we look back at ancient engineering, some cultures were far more capable of harnessing what little the natural elements had to offer than what we were once aware. The world appears to be repetitive, both in technological achievement and in human character.

It is an odd reality that history teaches us to be better

people by example of doomed intention. Yet, as each millennium goes by we seem as lost as ever. If civilizations have existed and risen to awe inspiring heights, why is it we seem just as much at the mercy of our baser instincts as we always have? History is ripe with examples of human frailty and the inevitable destruction of ourselves, even as our philosophies do their best to elevate us.

As many Eastern cultures embrace the experience of life and how to be at harmony with the world around us, other societies, such as those of the West, rush toward something far to the contrary. It is as if we are racing toward our very own end, eager for it to all finally come about.

Ancient cultures and lost civilizations have shown us to be full of knowledge that equals—perhaps even transcends—that of our present. Many of those past peoples surely felt they had reached a grandiose level in their time, much as we feel today. As if to reflect our temporary state, they eventually vanished from the earth, leaving only ruins behind.

If there was ever an example for a culture that has withstood time while continuously existing in harmony with the world around them, it is most likely Australian Aborigines.

This culture has never found a need to evolve beyond the deep connection they keep with the land around them, as well as the universe that holds them. Extremely spiritual, Aborigines are said to possess powers of clairvoyance, wherein they can sense if something is wrong with one another over miles of separation. From a certain point of view, it is said they possess such abilities due to their sparse lifestyle. Not normally prone to carrying cellphones around in the 'outback', such telepathic ability could be developed out of necessity, more than anything else. It may be the very sort of ability we all have, but which is suppressed in our own culture due to it being replaced by technology.

Observers have noted that Aborigines have a great connection to what is known as 'The Dreaming', which they rely upon in order to visit the 'Creation Period', during which their world was manifested by the 'Ancestral Beings' (see Appendix, Australian Aborigine Spiritualism, for more). Since the Creation Period is viewed as the beginning of everything, The Dreaming is often used to travel back to those beginnings in order to be one with the Ancestral Beings. It is at the Creation Period where all the information pertaining to the origin of the world is contained. This model is quite similar to that of the holographic universe, wherein physicists speculate all the information to our physical world is stored in a 2-dimensional existence and projected as part of our 3-dimensional reality.

In the end, The Dreaming is the place where every person exists for all eternity. It is where they existed before life and it is where they will exist after death. The Dreaming is the gateway to the astral plane, through which Aborigines travel to revisit the world from where they came during a long forgotten period.

There are civilizations that were around thousands of years before us, which we simply can not rationalize by our current standards. Some of them did reach levels that would seem impossible, based on what we know of them.

They certainly did not invent the microchip, nor did they invent jet or rocket engines (at least, we have never found any such evidence). As far as we know, there did not exist hand-held wireless devices with which to communicate, nor did they engineer a basic vehicle in which to get around (other than the horse and carriage, half of which is reliant on another animal's willingness to transport them).

How could such cultures have thrived for so long while seemingly having so little?

Those ancient peoples apparently developed an understanding that brought them in close relation to the wonders of the universe while using some of the most primitive means available. Yet, how they manipulated those means remains much of a mystery today.

Great pillars of stone have been erected through lesser cycles in such combination that they have seemingly opened up doorways to better understanding, and communing with, the universe. How these structures could be built remains an engineering marvel, considering those cultures did not possess the diesel churning monsters we now have for building our great towers of posterity. Scientists and professors are still attempting to unravel the mysteries of the the Great Pyramid of Giza, Stonehenge, and Puma Punku, to name some of the more controversial ruins of our world.

Ancient and lost civilizations are striking in what they have left behind. There is evidence all over the world that reveal technological artifacts that are similar in principal to a number of our own modern achievements. Yet, many of today's comparable items were only developed in the past 200 years, during the Industrial Revolution. One would have to wonder how, for instance, 2,000 year old batteries could be discovered in Baghdad, Iraq. A 2,000 year old computer, known as the Antikythera Mechanism, was built by the Greeks around the time of 150 BC. It was able to calculate astronomical changes and incorporated features that rival modern timepieces. In 132 AD, a Chinese inventor named Zhang Heng apparently created the world's first seismoscope. It is purported that recreations of the design have indeed been able to detect actual earthquakes.

During the year of 1898, an odd artifact was excavated from the tomb of Padiimen, near the Saqqara Pyramid, Egypt's oldest of pyramids. The artifact resembled a bird but was odd in that even though the front was shaped like the head of an avian creature, the wings were closer to the design of a modern airplane, or airfoil. The rear end was also reminiscent of an airplane rudder, being vertical rather than the horizontal shape of a feathered tail. Though there was no horizontal stabilizer, researchers have speculated that because the rudder was notched on top, this may be evidence of a horizontal stabilizer having once been affixed to it.

The man who discovered what became known as the Saqqara Bird, Dr. Khalil Messiha, built a replica and added a stabilizer to the tail. He claimed the bird had aerodynamic qualities similar to modern planes. Later, in 2006, Simon Sanderson, who had a background in aerodynamics, also built a replica and tested it in a wind tunnel. He found that the bird indeed exhibited lift capabilities of four times its weight.

Did this mean ancient Egyptians used to fly in larger models of this same design, in which a person could pilot what appears to have been an early glider?

Because it is believed there did not exist powered

aircraft in ancient Egypt it was theorized that if early gliders did exist they may have been launched with a type of catapult, much in the way modern gliders are launched from high hilltops by way of a bungee cord.

Given these technologies, which existed thousands of years ago, perhaps the existence of how such places as Puma Punku (located at Tiahuanaco) could have come to exist makes a bit more sense.

Constructed in Bolivia by predecessors of the Inca near Lake Titicaca and along the Andes Mountains, Puma Punku is estimated to have suddenly appeared around 300 AD. The inhabitants then disappeared about 500 years later. No one knows exactly who built the city, from where the inhabitants came, or where they went afterward. All that is known is the construction that was left behind, which employed sandstone blocks weighing up to 65 tons; the largest being around 130 metric tons. Those blocks came from one quarry 10 miles away and another that was 50 miles from the building site. One would wonder how such humungous stones could have been carried in an age before the horse and buggy had even come into existence. Bearing no chisel marks, how the stones were shaped also remains a mystery, as does the technology for how they were set together.

The exact age of Puma Punku seems to be a topic of debate as some archeologists put it at less than 2,000 years old, whereas others place it at 3,000 years due to the age of artifacts found at the site. One estimate (and a far departure from the above), conducted by Arthur Posnansky in 1945, actually puts the age at over 14,000 BC. Today, that estimate remains controversial, to say the least. In fact, there appears to be much controversy over all the estimates for how old Puma Punku truly is.

Sacsayhuamán was built by Incas between 1438 and 1471 AD and is situated near the city of Cuzco in Peru. Its walls are made of boulders that weigh up to 140 tons and joined so precisely that not even the thinnest object can penetrate the joints, even though no mortar was used. Archeologists remain mystified at how the walls were constructed using these huge megaliths.

Stonehenge, being a much older ruin of ancient construction which dates back to somewhere between 3,100 and 2,800 BC, results in further questions. It remains a mystery as to how the huge outer stones, known as 'sarsens', were carried and constructed, each one weighing 25 tons.

We merely assume past civilizations were much lesser developed than ours. Yet, we see evidence all around that those cultures were at least aware of our world in the same way we are today. While their technology may have varied from ours, they certainly seemed as knowledgeable as we about such things as construction and architecture, as well as astronomy and navigation. It would appear to make sense that we all go through a cultural growth, become great civilizations which thrive for hundreds, or thousands, of years, only to eventually topple so that we might begin somewhere else all over again.

Cultures of the Far East, such as China, have existed for thousands of years—4,000 years of written history and up to 8,000 years when taking into account the ruins of ancient sites. China is regarded as one of the great ancient civilizations, with many technological achievements coming from that time. Using fairly rudimentary means, other ancient cultures like the Mayans and Anasazi erected great structures and cities that seemed in tune with their world that we, today, are hard pressed to meet, even with our current technology.

What seems especially striking is how modern science has recently been showing models of the universe that ancient philosophies have talked about for thousands of years. How could those peoples have known things so long ago that our own culture is only discovering now? It prompts enough pause to wonder if we have already gone through such discoveries tens of thousands of years prior to this point.

We see evidence that civilizations have flourished for thousands of years before us, have apparently mastered an understanding of their environment and have then finally vanished. This pattern seems to repeat over and over throughout history, especially for those cultures that seem much more technologically advanced for their era.

It is as if we are only meant to go so far as a people before we seem to get ahead of ourselves. Once we are at the point that our struggles seem to disappear, or we seem to evolve too far, whether intellectually or technologically, it is as if someone wipes the board clean and starts it all over again, right from the lowest beginnings.

7

UFOs and Mothman

Not only is the universe stranger than we
imagine, it is stranger than we *can* imagine.

- Sir Arthur Eddington

Every culture has developed their own mythology
throughout the ages. What is mythology but a particular
peoples' way of describing their reality through various
stories and symbols. No matter how old or how young a
culture may be, there are usually tales of fantastic
happenings that have been handed down over generations.

We currently find ourselves with a host of similar
stories, ranging from such things as Bigfoot to ghosts that
haunt our lives and homes. Unidentified Flying Objects
(UFOs) have been one of the more predominant
phenomenon and one that appears to remain forever

elusive. Are they something to be taken seriously or just more folklore? Whether UFOs are real or imagined, or some form of psychological manifestation of our conscious mind, they are certainly real enough to have been taken seriously by governments of a number of countries, not the least of which has been that of the USA.

Clearly, the military has had interactions with this sort of aerial phenomenon, as have civil branches of aviation and numerous citizens. Reports have been taken seriously enough that the United States Air Force spent years investigating the phenomenon on a case-by-case basis, most popularly known as Project Blue Book (before finally 'closing the book' on it in December, 1969). Currently, the government appears to have given these sightings less priority, though our military certainly remains aware of them.

Sightings of UFOs began as early as the 1940s. They became much more prevalent throughout the 1950s and 1960s, quite possibly due to the popular culture of the time. The growth of science fiction literature and movies depicting alien invasions led to a public craze in the United States, which culminated in a nationwide panic when Orson Welles broadcast an adaptation of HG Well's famous story, *War of the Worlds*, over the radio on October 30, 1938.

Since then, the public has largely viewed UFOs as spacecraft—saucer or cigar shaped and, later, triangular—controlled by alien visitors from other worlds. The early space programs of NASA during the 1960s certainly helped to shape that popular mindset. But, if we look at some of the cases of UFO encounters, it seems these 'spaceships' do not always behave like mechanical devices. Quite often they transform into other objects or are viewed in completely conflicting ways from person to person when multiple witnesses are involved.

A classic example is a series of incidents that occurred at Rendlesham Forest over a period of several days. The details of what follows is taken from documents and articles detailing those events.

From December 26 to 29, in 1980, US and UK air force personnel observed UFO phenomenon in the woods that separated two military air bases in the United Kingdom—RAF US Air Force Bentwaters and RAF US Air Force Woodbridge. During one of the encounters, a triangular craft was spotted in Rendlesham Forest by two US airmen, Jim Penniston and John Burrows. Penniston actually got close enough to touch the craft before it silently moved up into the sky and disappeared. During another night, Lieutenant-Colonel Charles Halt observed a red, sun-like orb through the trees. It pulsed like a blinking eye and threw off glowing particles of what appeared to be molten metal, though no traces of the material could later be found anywhere on the ground. Finally, the light exploded silently into five white objects and quickly disappeared. Shortly after this occurred the lights were seen by other base personnel who described them flying into the sky and making sharp, angular movements at high speed.

This sort of bizarre behavior is common to a number of similar sightings, though Rendlesham Forest is clearly one of the most high profile cases in recent history. That each encounter by the three main observers were described differently is also striking. Penniston described touching what seemed to be a triangular shaped craft that flew away immediately afterward, while Halt described it as a pulsing light. John Burrows later recounted the object as something completely different from either of those descriptions—what might be described as an extra-dimensional manifestation—even though he observed it at the same time as did his colleague, Jim Penniston.

Nonsensical encounters with faceless men dressed in black, who are sometimes described as having no face, also appear to be linked to UFO sightings. Though wearing dark suits, such figures are often described as otherworldly.

The strange nature of such encounters is more reminiscent of something commonly experienced in a dream state, rather than a waking reality. Yet, such bizarre confrontations have been reported as far back as the year 1561, during a historic occurrence which took place in Nuremberg, Germany. During that particular occasion, multiple witnesses described the sky (at daybreak) being filled with strange objects such as spheres, crescents, crosses, a black spear and cylinders from which several smaller spheres emerged and darted about the sky.

Many sightings that are investigated by UFO researchers are never reported to the media, but a number of them have striking similarities, such as the shape the encounter takes. Instead of being an obvious craft that descends from the sky, the object often forms on the spot and then morphs into something the observer seems to expect. It is as if the object becomes a manifestation of the observer's conscious mind. If the witness is expecting some type of UFO encounter, it becomes just that. If multiple witnesses are present, they will sometimes interact differently with the phenomenon manifesting before them. This explains why some observers will see nothing while others see classic UFO scenarios unfold. The encounter may continue to fit the parameters of a UFO experience, but the details and physical attributes can alter quite radically among witnesses. The mere fact that many encounters involve the object changing shape, becoming brighter and then disappearing altogether, like a light being shut off, suggests such possibilities as an altered reality or a supernatural experience.

As researchers look into such non-popularized aspects of UFO encounters as those described above, some of them —physicist and author, Jacques Vallee, being among the notables—are now leaning towards an altered reality that involves conscious perception as an explanation for the phenomenon. Whether this involves a psychic or an inter-dimensional experience, or a combination of both, is still up for debate. Still, when faced with a choice of the phenomenon being either the result of an altered state of consciousness or a spaceship traveling thousands of light years to visit us, the more plausible explanation becomes an altered psychological sense of reality.

Looking at the numbers and placing a bet on pure probability, it seems logical to assume there is other intelligent life in the universe beyond our own. There are several hundred billion stars in just our own galaxy, the Milky Way. With the billions of galaxies we see, and do not yet see, one would be prone to think by mere probability that we are not the only planet throughout all those possible solar systems which may harbor life.

All the observable galaxies we see around us are those close enough for light to have traveled to our world in the time the earth has existed. Since there are stars and galaxies older than our own, we can assume there may be more advanced civilizations out there that must have surely developed interstellar travel by now. Still, the thought of such a capability seems utterly fantastic by our own standards and what we have come to know of physics and its associated limitations.

Despite this, there remains a hopeful element that something akin to interstellar travel may still be possible.

As fantastic as it may sound, work is purportedly being conducted in an attempt to develop a warp drive that circumvents the established limitation of light speed.

In 2012, a NASA engineer, Dr. Harold White, allegedly began leading a team of engineers and scientists at NASA's Eagleworks facility in designing a ship that would actually travel faster than light. It does so, theoretically, by expanding space-time behind it while contracting space-time in front. The technique exploits a loophole in the law of no object being able to travel faster than light, as developed by Albert Einstein in his Special Theory of Relativity. While local objects can not travel through space faster than the speed of light, space-time, itself, can theoretically move at any velocity. This is one of the suppositions put forth by Big Bang theorists who speculate the universe expanded faster than light when the cataclysmic event supposedly took place.

Since no conclusive evidence has yet come to light as a result of these apparently fringe NASA experiments, the technology remains below the mainstream and out of reach for the time being.

Even with this revelation in possibly realizing interstellar travel at some point, the likelihood of other beings traveling to our world from distant planets remains unlikely. In all our efforts and observations so far, it remains a hit and miss scenario when it comes to determining which planets in our own galaxy may support life.

The manifestation of UFO encounters may be real—plenty of physical evidence has purportedly been collected over decades of investigations—but some pundits are still leaning toward alternate dimensions and higher realities as the source, rather than the phenomenon being that of visitors from distant worlds. Of all those billions of galaxies and the billions of stars within each one, it would still seem completely coincidental if anyone else discovered our whereabouts as a result of their interstellar travels.

From my own perspective, each time I have seen strange aerial phenomenon and become intrigued by it, never have I been overcome with the sense I was witnessing an alien visitation from another planet. I would experience a certain awe, but I always felt what I was seeing was something quite departed from such stereotypical presumption.

Even as sightings of UFO phenomenon appear in the tabloids as many people cackle over the preposterous indulgence of a reckless implication, there remains another faction who take the matter quite seriously.

I have friends and relatives who have worked in our military's air force and have been posted within various radar stations. Tasked with the responsibility of tracking what we believe to be our secure skies, there appear to be some strange events taking place, of which many of us are hardly aware.

One acquaintance, manning a military radar station,

recounted a number of occurrences wherein strange targets, commonly referred to as 'bogies', would appear on the radar screen without any authorized reason in being there. Unable to identify the object and subsequently interpreting the target as a potential threat, fighter jets were usually scrambled to intercept the object. Even as the fighters were closing in, their own guidance systems would be unable to lock onto the target. Invariably, the strange object would zip away from the intercept at incomprehensible speeds, leaving the guardians of our skies merely shaking their heads and burying the incident as a non-occurrence.

The point is that our many nations' air forces have been quite aware of such phenomenon for a protracted period. Such encounters are usually dismissed out of embarrassment—no one wants to admit there is something going on which they can not explain. An air force is designed to protect its nation's airspace, after all. Such a task may seem redundant when the military branches can not even identify something that may be a threat, or may not. The simple matter that they are unable to ascertain even that much is enough cause for alarm.

This is most likely why most military segments of our government would prefer not to discuss such unidentifiable aberrations. It is apparently more dignified to deny the existence of something that can not be explained than to admit its existence while, at the same time, having to confess there is no clear way to deal with it.

I believe our governments and our military forces remain completely aware of UFO phenomenon. It could very well be we have come to realize what we are seeing is not at all alien visitors from other worlds but are manifestations of our earthly condition with which we have probably coexisted throughout history. As much as any strange phenomenon exists within our culture and among our folklore, such things as bright lights in the sky and objects that behave without regard to our own physical laws remain as much a part of our mythology to this day. It is something we have simply learned to live with, just as our ancestors learned to live with specters they came to define as gods, angels and demons that would occasionally invade their own reality.

I do admit to having some strange experiences which have involved UFO encounters. It should not be misinterpreted that by the term, UFO, this signified some alien spacecraft. The object was simply something I could not identify while it was moving about the sky. I did, however, have a profound sense of it being something other than a typical aerial occurrence.

A strange event took place, about ten years prior to this writing, at my country estate home. The property has a number of acres and is cut off from neighboring homes, as it is surrounded by hundred foot tall spruce trees. It was during the night and I was sitting down at the large pond toward the back of the property. The air was clear and a host of stars peppered the evening sky.

About thirty minutes into my nightly reflections, I noticed a very bright star off to the southeast. I thought, momentarily, it was odd that I had not noticed it before. Stars appear to move slowly at night as the earth completes each revolution. However, after close to an hour it was still in the same spot, shining brightly. Just as I began to feel uncomfortable with it hovering for so long, seemingly out of place from everything else, it finally started to move quite noticeably.

The star (which was now clearly not a star at all) began to descend slowly toward me. It stopped and hovered for a while, then began to move up again in the opposite direction until it became stationary over a line of trees to the south. It made no sound, appeared to be close and had no strobe or anti-collision lights, as any aircraft would. Then, somewhat anticlimactically, after about half an hour from when it began to initially move toward me, it just winked off and disappeared.

The object was clearly not an aircraft. I am used to having airplanes fly over my area on a constant basis. I have had enough experience flying as both a pilot and a passenger that I knew full well it was not an aircraft of any sort. I also see satellites and meteors all the time and this was also neither of those, nor was it a flare, as military aircraft sometimes drop during exercises.

The following month I had another experience quite similar to this one while sitting out on my deck during another clear night.

This time a white light was hovering above the trees directly to the south. After I began to wonder if this was a star or something else, the object began moving toward me. It hovered for a while, then began to ascend, moving slowly toward the west with no accompanying sound. Eventually, it simply vanished from view as if someone had turned off a light, just like the other one had done prior to that.

Even the smallest airplanes that pass by make a sound, but this particular object produced nothing. To this day I can not lump it in with any of the normally occurring aerial displays I freely observe every night, man-made or natural, so I am not sure exactly what it was. Thus, it remained unidentified.

Though UFOs have certainly been a dominant theme for hundreds of years, they are not the only aberration that causes us to question the meaning of our reality. Something that has become part of our societies' popular mythology, of late, has been the phenomenon of Mothman. This has largely come to light just over the past half-century, or so, though some interpretations could have it dating back hundreds of years.

The most well known sightings of Mothman to have happened recently occurred in Point Pleasant, West Virginia, from a period stretching from the month of November, 1966, to December, 1967. The sightings, which were reported by multiple witnesses over that time, apparently came to an end after the Silver Bridge connecting West Virginia to Ohio collapsed on December 15, 1967.

According to some witnesses, Mothman appeared as what they believed to be a harbinger of terrible things that were about to happen. But is Mothman an actual, physical being or is it just another manifestation of our conscious mind and our connection to a universal collective?

From witness descriptions of Mothman, a clear impression emerges of how extremely alien the creature appears to observers. It is alien in the sense that eyewitness accounts describe it as being nothing even remotely resembling a human being. It is apparently not even humanoid, a point emphasized by its strange bird-like wings and eyes that seem nestled in the chest area of the body, leaving it with no distinguishable head. It has legs but not arms and stands seven to eight feet tall, by witness accounts, and its body is dark. Usually, observers notice the eyes before anything else, which are red and glowing. Anyone seeing Mothman for the first time would surely be convinced they were witnessing a monster from a nightmare, not even closely man-like.

It is a far departure from the typical aliens encountered on the latest episodes of *Star Trek*, where each one looks exactly like a human, except for an odd color or an out of place appendage. Quite contrary to Hollywood's notion of what an alien might look like, Mothman is something far departed and splintered from our own sense of reality.

This creature certainly fits the definition of a supernatural being, more demonic in appearance than angelic and ready to scare the hell out of us at any moment of its choosing. It never seems to come to us with good news. It only appears to precede impending death and doom. We are powerless to stop what we perceive as prognostications, leaving us to merely witness the tragedies that come about following the appearance of this otherworldly being.

Like some alien visitors, wherein witnesses have claimed their abductors appeared in human form, but were somehow not quite right—not as human as observers thought they should have been—some have also described encounters around Mothman sightings wherein an unearthly being has approached them in human form. Again, the witness describes speaking with the being, even though they notice something strange and out of place about the overall appearance of the disturbing visitor. In fact, while many observers report their encounters being as bizarre and nonsensical as a dream, they seem to accept what is happening during their experience as if it were as real as anything else. This could be due to their conscious perception of reality being altered during the encounter, as it would similarly be during a dream.

It might make sense that Mothman and aliens would appear so strange and disguised to us if they were truly beings from beyond our physical world. If they were so departed from us that they were not of our known universe, but existed within some further dimension, they would not resemble anything similar to ourselves. Our minds would likely not be able to process their presence in a way that would make sense. This may very well be why so many strange visitations occur in the form of a human, although an oddly disturbing human, at that. Anything else would quite possibly drive us mad for our inability to understand it. If another universe were to come in contact with ours from another plane of reality, it would quite likely be too out of place to interpret by our accepted standards. Indeed, the two states of reality could simply not exist in the same place in such a way that would be natural or make some degree of sense in our own mind.

Mothman appears to be another manifestation of an alternate reality that exists beyond our own. Based on some theories, it is a being that sees events that occur in our own world from a different perspective. Perhaps what is a future event to us is actually a present moment to Mothman.

Is such a notion all that far-fetched?

Thousands of years of recorded history have already suggested we seem to exist between a world of plausible reality and ridiculous absurdity. Given such extremes in what we have come to accept as real, should we not have the mental fortitude to accept the possibility of existent realities outside what we have so far witnessed in our own?

A popular theory of Mothman, put forth by paranormal researcher, John Keel, in his 1975 book, *The Mothman Prophecies*, is that it is a being that comes from an alternate reality or a parallel universe. We are no longer potentially dealing with just extraterrestrials; we now have 'ultra-terrestrials' with which to contend. As modern physics has shown, it is quite possible there are higher dimensions of existence and realities beyond our own.

Some of those witnesses who have been exposed to Mothman have endured strange, physical after-effects. Subsequently, doctors have not been able to explain many of these ailments suffered by the witness, let alone how they may have been caused.

Consider a person from our own existence coming in contact with a being from another reality, or higher dimension we have yet to discover. If two, differing dimensions were to interact at a juncture that does not physically allow for both to exist within the same space at the same time, there would likely be understandable side-effects suffered by those who are not designed to exist within those two, separate realities. This could be the reason for the weird physical maladies doctors are unable to diagnose after Mothman encounters, as well as a number of UFO experiences.

It has been proposed by John Keel that such things as Mothman, UFOs, angels and men in black could all be manifestations that are solely interpreted by our culture and time in history. It could be that such phenomena are merely a supernatural condition of our world that has always existed alongside us, as historic folklore and mythology has often indicated. Sometimes these extra-dimensional beings cross over to our world or are perceived by those with unique abilities, presenting themselves in such ways that we are able to briefly interact with them.

It is sometimes laughable how easily we explain away the inexplicable, simply by equating such experiences to bizarre, cliché scenarios that have largely been perpetuated by Hollywood and the media. That the ultimate resolution to our existence and all the conflicts we experience through our lives should be diminished to a popular media driven soundbite seems a bit sad, as if there were no better epitaphs offered by a more insightful poet.

Clearly, we do not seem meant to glean some profound meaning from these unearthly encounters, least of all be able to rationally explain them. It seems entirely designed that none are meant to leave us with a discernible clue as to where these experiences originate. Possibly someone, or something, in whatever form it may take, is doing what it can to prepare us for what is beyond our current realm of perception.

Whatever the origin of these encounters, all bear a strikingly similar pattern. In each case, we are taken out of our present understanding of what is real and we are transposed into a separate reality. Within that encounter, for however brief the moment may be, we are confronted with objects and symbols that challenge our conceived notion of what our reality may truly be. We come into contact with an element that is beyond our understanding. It is only after we are confronted with this changed reality that our own existence begins to unravel.

Since these experiences occur within an altered state, it

is understandable that our physical bodies would begin to break down under the conflict of one reality within another.

Whether the physical ailments come by way of Mothman, UFOs, or even by way of encounters with heavenly gods, which have momentarily come into our world, they tend to leave us with scars or illnesses following such encounters. We are clearly not built to walk unharmed through the higher dimensions of our alternate realities without suffering the affect of such a journey.

Yet, despite the waking notion that there may be higher planes of existence, we should feel a euphoria in knowing those alternate realities dwell hand-in-hand as we walk through our lives, seeing we can simply reach out and touch the very fabric that separates one plane of existence from the next. If we have learned nothing else from these otherworldly encounters, the one takeaway is that those fleeting signs of a higher existence are telling a number of us there is another reality far beyond our current understanding. Perhaps we are all destined to eventually find that place where angels, aliens and Mothman walk freely among us, waiting to be discovered.

8

The Probability of Quantum Mechanics
(and Alternate Realities)

If you think you understand quantum mechanics,
you don't understand quantum mechanics.

- Richard Feynman

Quantum mechanics, and its associated theories, offers us converging possibilities that would explain some of the more bizarre realities of our existence and what death may actually represent. Niels Bohr, one of the most timely physicists our past century has known, actually stated that, "Anyone who is not shocked by quantum theory has not understood it.".

Our natural world has defining qualities of its basic order, which we can usually understand easily enough. This is what we know as our macro world—the one we see all around us through our daily interactions. Beyond that is a layer that resides below the atomic level. This is where things become more convoluted.

Let us consider that the physical world is not a static existence. It is an unnatural form of being we seem to endure in order to pursue a dynamic reality. Philosophies that are imbedded in a number of cultures believe our fluctuating consciousness moves in and out of an astral plane, to which we are bound even after death. Seeing this first hand upon coming into the world has caused me to question reality and seek explanations through various forms, whether they be spiritual, scientific or an evolution of both. The science of physics is really nothing more than a way to define the nature of our reality. Spirituality attempts to explain what we have not been able to realize through science. Yet, both can be said to characterize our reality by the way we see it, or by the way we perceive it.

In a nutshell, quantum mechanics is the study of our universe—our natural world and all it encompasses—on the smallest scale we know (with the possible exception of string theory). There was a time we believed the atom was as small as things got. Quantum theory has shown that the universe is composed of particles that are even smaller than the atom. More to the point, some of these quantum objects have been observed to exist in stranger states than we normally see within our own world. At the same time, quantum theory opens the possibility that higher dimensions quite likely exist beyond what we typically experience on a personal level.

The physics of quanta (plural of quantum) has shown some particles exist in a subjective state, which is sometimes affected by probability. If we do not observe them, they may exist in a different form, or perhaps not at all. This measurable characteristic has been proved through experimentation and has given rise to the concept that the universe and reality may only exist for as long as there is someone, or something, to observe it. In a similar way, we could say our conscious awareness manifests our own reality.

Objects (or particles) within the quantum world can exhibit bizarre characteristics, such as spinning both clockwise and counterclockwise simultaneously. Entanglement is a characteristic wherein a quantum particle that is affected a certain way can simultaneously cause those same effects in another object separated by a comparatively large distance. Therefore, it is entangled. Quantum theory also gives rise to a specific particle existing in more than one place at the same time.

One of the most famous experiments that proved a quantum object, such as an electron, can exhibit the characteristics of both a wave and a particle, is the double-slit experiment.

The Delayed Choice Experiment, as it was termed, was postulated by John Archibald Wheeler in 1978. The experiment showed that an electron would act as a particle when traveling through one slit, but when two slits were introduced the electron began to act like a wave. This was observed by an interference pattern that emerged on a metal plate beyond the slits, upon which it was expected just one or two lines of electrons would show up on the plate where they had impacted. Quite to the contrary, however, there were a number of lines which indicated the electrons were acting as waves when passing through both slits. The spaces between the pattern on the metal plate were a result of the areas where the waves had interacted with one another and had canceled each other out. Where they had not interacted with one another, the lines appeared on the metal plate to form the interference pattern. Physicists tried to cancel out this effect by firing just one electron through one of the two slits at a time. Once again, the interference pattern emerged, which led to the conclusion that the electron was going through both slits at once, thus acting like a wave.

In search of an answer for this seemingly dual nature of the electron particle, a measuring device was placed close to where the electrons were being fired through the two slits. The unexpected result was that the electrons went back to acting like particles and merely produced two lines on the metal plate where it was expected that the interference pattern displaying many lines would appear once more. It was clear that by introducing a device to observe and measure the electrons, they reverted to acting like particles, rather than waves.

It is this act of observing the particles that causes the strange and seemingly irrational behavior of quantum matter. Instead of acting the same way every time, the quantum matter appears to change its behavior for no other reason than being observed.

This strange set of possible outcomes demonstrated by the experiment has led others to a theory that everything we experience may be in an illusory state and only coalesces into what we know as our reality once we have observed it, or otherwise measured it. This has led to the extraordinary postulation that if none of us were around to observe anything, the universe and our reality within it may not even exist (at least, not in the form we understand today).

Such a proposition is clearly a very contradictory and somewhat scary prospect for anyone dependent on static realities to validate their existence. Yet, this scientific discovery, along with a number of successive experiments, seems to be pointing us toward an inescapable conclusion.

Even in 2015, following an experiment at the Australian National University employing Wheeler's delayed-choice experiment, physicist, Dr. Andrew Truscott, stated that his experiment "...proves that measurement is everything" and that "...reality does not exist if you are not looking at it."

All this is just the beginning of the strangeness that exists within the quantum world.

The notion that the same particle can exist in many different places at the same time has given rise to alternative realities existing through higher dimensions that exist alongside our own.

A Texas Tech University professor of chemistry, named Bill Poirier, formulated a theory that was published in 2010, called *Many Interacting Worlds*. Essentially, the theory postulates that small particles from parallel worlds —what we could describe as alternate realities—are close enough to our own world that they manage to come into ours and interact with us from time to time. This could explain what creates the strange behavior of quantum matter wherein, for one thing, the same object can appear to exist in several places at once.

The theory has been examined through symposiums and lectures, as well as through published papers. Currently, the theory has much support from other notable figures within the physics community who agree with the math behind it. Mathematics and experimentation has resulted in other famous physicists accepting the multiple worlds idea—what has been coined the 'multiverse' theory —as a very real possibility.

Beyond just these prospects, quantum theory also allows an object to move along simultaneous paths and end up in different places at once. This is what is known as 'quantum superposition'. If we observe the object, however, the superposition breaks down and follows just one trajectory, and one time-line.

Quantum mechanics, along with our very reality, appears to be largely dependent on our presence and our ability to witness it, or even, dare I say, conjure it.

For a long time I have thought of the brain as simply an organic interface that allows our consciousness to interact with our known, physical world. Decades ago, scientists attested to much of our brain being untapped. That the brain is not often used to its full potential offers the possibility there may be higher functions that allow us to interact with those alternate realities in ways that sometimes appear random or accidental. When we think we have seen something unearthly, or ethereal, it could be the less used portion of our brain that is actually allowing us to interface with alternative realities. Science has shown (at least on paper) these extra-dimensional worlds to exist alongside our own.

Perhaps this is why Mothman seems to manifest tentatively, while not fully existing within the scope of our own world. It could be this creature is a being who dwells in a higher dimension of existence than our own, thus giving it the ability to see events we have not yet witnessed in our world, but which Mothman has already seen take place while pushing up against our own reality. The same could be true of such things as UFOs and otherworldly phenomenon with which we occasionally come into contact but are unable to logically explain. Perhaps this is why such occurrences would appear to be more accurately described as psychological, or paranormal, events. That part of our misunderstood brain may be responsible for allowing a conscious awareness of those things that exist beyond the normal perception of our 3-dimensional world.

If this is a scientific explanation for realities that exist beyond our own, maybe death is merely a transcendence from this lower state of reality into a higher plane of existence; an existence within a reality of further dimensions among the 'multiverse'.

It could be we are already existing in a higher dimension than the one in which we were before, or that we are existing within more than one reality at the same time. If the holographic universe theory is correct in its postulation that we are nothing more than 2-dimensional beings who are projecting ourselves into a 3-dimensional reality, this would already be evidence that we can exist in multiple realities at the same time. When all the information and energy that is responsible for our existence in one world dissipates and moves unencumbered to the next, death or non-existence in this world is the means by which we move into that other reality.

Just as we may project ourselves through the holographic universe, dream states could be an alternate form of conscious awareness as we project ourselves into another possible existence. Ancient Egyptians believed this much in equating dream states to the afterlife.

The Probability of Quantum Mechanics

What does all this really tell us about quantum mechanics?

The most fascinating thing about quantum mechanics is that the scientific theory is so bizarre and prone to myriad possibilities that it sometimes seems it may be the only rational way to explain something quite irrational. That the science of quantum matter appears contradictory, at times, could offer the greatest probability in explaining confounding possibilities.

Quantum mechanics is an integral area of scientific study which, combined with classical physics, forms the basis of modern physics today. Throw in some string theory and anything in the world seems possible.

The strange nature of quantum science is that much of its study and resultant experimentation is largely reliant on probability. A particular object or particle may exist in one point, at one time, but it may also exist at another point at the same time. Whereas a particular object may display mass and speed, only one can be measured at a time, while negating the ability to measure the other. Therefore, knowing the quantities of any particular object can never be certain, which gives rise to what is known as the 'uncertainty principle'.

As if this were not enough, from that point quantum mechanics only becomes more peculiar and uncertain. That a quantum object may only exist through observation causes many to recoil or become angry over such lack of clarity. This uncertainty, which governs particular aspects of quantum behavior, gave rise to Albert Einstein declaring, "I like to think the moon is there even if I am not looking at it".

An analogy to this idea of things not truly existing until

they are observed is the cat in the box—a thought experiment known as 'Schrodinger's Cat'. It is named after Austrian physicist, Erwin Schrodinger, who posited the theory in 1935. This thought experiment became known as the Copenhagen interpretation for quantum superposition, wherein more than one outcome can exist at the same time.

The experiment works by first placing a cat inside a lead box. A degradable canister of cyanide is placed in the box along with the cat and the box is then sealed. At this point we do not know whether the canister has degraded and released the cyanide, or whether the cat is now dead or alive. We can assume that if the canister breaks down the cat would be dead. If the cyanide canister does not break down, we suppose the cat is alive. The point is we can not know for sure which outcome has materialized. According to quantum theory, the cat exists in both states—quantum superposition—alive and dead at the same time for as long as the condition remains uncertain. It is only after the box is opened and we see that the cat is dead or alive that the superposition breaks down and the condition finds its solution.

Direct observation is required for the probability of any particular outcome to manifest itself. Then again, if the cat were discovered to be dead it could also be alive in a parallel universe, wherein the multiverse offers all possibilities.

The concept of many parallel worlds has become seriously considered by a number of well respected physicists, to the point they have written best-selling books on the topic. Because quantum objects have a probability of existing in many states (possibly even many dimensions) these alternate realities are theorized to exist alongside our own.

Quantum mechanics is only a doorway to realizing how weird physical reality happens to be. That being said, the above is, by no means, intended to be a comprehensive explanation of quantum mechanics. It takes years of study to fully understand its dynamics. This very brief overview is merely meant to demonstrate the quirky and subjective character of the natural objects that exist within our world. Because of this, we could argue that the nature of our world is equally quirky and subject to interpretation.

It is difficult to go from quantum mechanics, in its most simple definition of being the study of very small objects at the subatomic level, to all the possibilities it offers in philosophical terms. To consider that some quantum objects only exist due to our conscious awareness of them comes across as very existential. Considering that quantum mechanics has been around for about 100 years now, one would think we would understand it better. It has, however, led to many breakthroughs in science, such as LEDs, lasers, transistors and the microprocessors found in computers.

While I do not dare pretend to be an expert in quantum science—the equations are daunting, to say the least—it does offer intriguing possibilities in alternate realities and parallel universes. Much of our physical world still remains a very tantalizing mystery.

Coincidentally, when I was a teenager in public school, I began to imagine there was another person who looked and acted just like me. I could not see that person, but I always felt they existed at the same time, in a different place. After a while, that spurred me onto the thought that other dimensions existed alongside our own which we could not see. I even went as far as telling some of my classmates and friends about the idea, most of whom understandably thought I was losing my mind.

It would be the next millennium before I would discover a growing number of physicists had developed similar beliefs and had then proved their theories on paper, or through empirical observation.

Partially due to this realization, I believe that deep down in our subconscious many of us are aware of things we do not even know we are. If we never truly die but keep changing from one state of consciousness to another, we are as infinite as the universe in its many different versions. We all carry the same knowledge but it may be more suppressed in some than in others. There are those of us who are simply more in tune with the mechanisms of our reality while others are more in tune to other aspects. Quantum mechanics and string theory allow for the possibility of infinity and circular time.

Some Eastern philosophies believe we can live 100,000 lives, or more, before we finally transform our conscious existence permanently—that thing which is often called enlightenment. I have wondered how any of us could live that many lives. Assuming we lived an average of thirty years in each life, that would mean the human race would be 3 million years old, unless that included life as an orangutang or a blade of grass. Then again, if time is circular and both past and present exist at the same moment, and in alternate dimensions, who can say for sure how long a recycled existence could really last. The passage of time in the death state is clearly not measurable in the same way it is in the land of the living. If Hinduism is correct and there are infinite universes and realities, and we can exist in all of them, perhaps the secrets of eternity are locked inside every one of us.

If we have truly been around forever, existing in different forms or repeating cycles of life and death, one would think that by now we surely would have picked up some hidden insight along the way. Those genius minds that transform and revolutionize how we think of things may be those people who have more retained knowledge than the rest of us. It is difficult to say for sure what is suppressed in all those subconscious minds?

9

The Land of the Living
and
The World of the Dead

There is a design for why we exist in quite the way we do. The reason for that design is simple, yet elegant.

A range of beliefs pervade, along with disbelief. We choose the one with which we feel most at ease. There is no right or wrong in that decision, but it is a choice that separates us and causes the splinter between one philosophical imperative and another. We are little more than expectations teetering on a precipice of possibility.

As much as I have suggested we all come into the world with an initial sense that physical existence is false, the majority of us are taken by the world's influence as it lulls us. Human beings have proved to be great adapters to harsh environments. It is our ability to adjust to our surroundings, without question, that makes us well suited for survival, apparently able to thrive within widely varying states of existence.

This is not by accident. After all, given the evidence of our predisposition to destroy ourselves, we seem to have a remarkable ability to rise out of the ashes and carry on with whatever new culture or civilization we see fit to impress upon this world in the wake of our latest, grand mistake. By pure example, we seem to purposely head toward self-destruction just so we can witness the result. This possibly comes out of nothing more than absolute curiosity. If we do not truly belong here, what better way to witness the trappings of physical temptation than by creating the very medium wherein we are free to watch it all fall apart, much to our amusement.

We are condemned to a painful existence. It is not for the sake of merely wasting time. There is a reason we create an environment of conflict. Without that influence over us, we would never have the opportunity to challenge it and grow into a greater awareness of ourselves. We are here for the wondrous purpose of embracing reality in its many forms and to feel that sense of being alive. Only when we are completely lost and without direction do those remarkable traits of the human soul come to light.

Many of us may have no idea why we are here, why we exist, or what purpose we could possibly lend, other than the very same reason many of our fellow mammals and critters are here.

It often seems the majority of our life in this world is to provide sustenance and a reason for others to live by our side, until that moment wherein our fellow savages realize they can not exist a moment longer without devouring our very own essence. For many, it appears we are fated to live alongside one another until that time comes to finally die and be faced with our awakening. Only once we truly realize our repetitive nature for what it is can we cast off such trappings and move on to a higher awareness.

We live in flux in order to grow into something more. It would be redundant if there were no greater good in our purpose than simply causing each other to doubt ourselves. If we all lived completely isolated from one another there would be no growth. Nothing would be learned from having that essential contact with each other. In the end we would return to pure spirit, no more than what we were when we came into life.

Physical reality is mystical and esoteric. The essence from which we were formed is divine and Elysian. If we are eternal beings, it would make sense that we should be aware of more than what we simply see around us. For many, that sense remains disguised as "a riddle, wrapped in a mystery, inside an enigma" (Winston Churchill's famous quote).

It may feel to many of us that this is all there is. Such an assumption remains flawed. Our consciousness moves back and forth between corporeal and ethereal reality, even while we are alive. The movements are usually subtle, but sometimes they are more disturbing than with what many of us may be comfortable.

49 Days in the Bardo

Many cultures have their own belief in what happens following death. Some are markedly similar in their overall description of what occurs to the soul, but with differing social bents. Tibetan Buddhism gives much attention to those going through the levels of death and various spiritual encounters, along with how to traverse the afterlife. It is through teachings that are offered in life that prepare a person to face what awaits them once they have passed into death.

What we experience in life, the expectations we develop and the kind of person we become, largely sets the tone for how we will deal with things that challenge us in our afterlife. In most cases we will likely dwell in limbo, within a dreamlike state that may leave many of us unaware we are even dead. Aspects of being disconnected from our physical domain will soon come to light as we are faced with frightening challenges. For those who are prepared and mentally honed to face whatever the Bardo of the afterlife throws at them, that experience may be short lived. Anyone who sees the death state for what it is should be able to transcend the physical world before spending much time in that place between death and birth.

The term, Bardo, is a Tibetan word which means, 'in between space', or 'between places'. This disembodied limbo could be equatable to the Catholic notion of purgatory. Essentially, it is a place where we linger as we await our self-imposed fate for the soul's next phase of its journey.

In Buddhist teachings of the Tibetan philosophy (one that is sometimes evident in other Eastern philosophies) the first stage of death is what Tibetan Buddhists call the Bardo of Dying. For many, this stage tends to pass quickly. It comes in such an instant that it most likely passes unnoticed. Within that moment, however, there is a rare chance to see pure consciousness for what it truly is. This can only be glimpsed for as long as the dead person is properly prepared and completely aware of what is happening to them. The person will be faced with the 'Clear Light', which is what ancient philosophies of the Far East refer to as 'naked consciousness'. If the Clear Light is recognized, the dead person will be able to transcend the constant cycle of death and rebirth, seeing the light as absolute truth and the reason for existence far beyond the physical realm. But, if the Clear Light is not recognized, fear takes over and the dead person remains in the Bardo to face the bizarre and confusing nature of the afterlife. There they do whatever they can to battle the confusion encountered among the nightmares of their hidden existence.

Once the person has moved into the Bardo of the afterlife—in Tibetan texts this is referred to as the Bardo of Experiencing Reality—they will spend a number of days encountering spiritual entities. These manifestations will present the opportunity for the dead person to enter the realms of enlightened beings. However, for those who have little awareness of such things, the dead person will often become disoriented and frightened as they encounter strange realities beyond their understanding. These ambassadors of the world beyond the physical are said to be accompanied by intense, blinding lights, as well as deafening sounds that will disorient and confuse the dead person. Such beings are said to possess an overwhelming brilliance that has the ability to terrify those who are easily frightened by such unearthly luminosity.

It is during these encounters with the spiritual beings that some visions will become appealing to the dead person as they stir up such familiar emotions as pride, aggression, or jealousy. Those negative thoughts can then lead the person into another world of negative life, or even a 'hell world'. If the dead person does become lured by such emotions, the deity who initially evoked them will quickly disappear, closing the opportunity for the person to enter their world and to also become an enlightened being.

For the first seven days of the Bardo, the dead person will encounter deities that are peaceful, but which will continue to be frightening to anyone who does not understand what is happening. A person who has been trained in life for what to expect in that deathly limbo will know their greatest strength toward transcendence is to recognize the light for what it is, along with the spiritual entities who follow. Negative emotions must be purged so that feelings of love can take their place in order to be accepted by the beings who now confront them. It is only through the rejection of negative emotions—emotions which likely pushed the dead person into the physical world in the first place—that the disembodied soul can move forward, rather than back into the perpetual cycle of physical life.

If none of the peaceful beings are embraced during the first seven days, the next seven days bring the angry and wrathful deities to confront the dead person as they continue to linger in the Bardo. There they will continue to struggle with their confusion. If the person was frightened by the first group of beings, they surely will not be any happier with the next onslaught of deities they must now face.

It is explained in the sacred texts that the person must stay focused and not allow emotions to take over the experience of encountering these spiritual beings, no matter how terrifying they may be. The person must try to realize that all the apparitions which are encountered in the Bardo of Experiencing Reality are reflections and projections of the person's own mind. If the person is able to stay focused and remain on the middle path between the two extremes of these encounters with the spiritual beings, they may still be able to move into the higher dimensions of the pure light realms.

Upon failing all encounters with these beings, up to the fourteenth day and unsuccessful in entering a spiritual state, the person then moves into the next Bardo of the afterlife. This is called the Bardo of Becoming. It is during this stage that the person's soul is largely without direction as it becomes victim to various emotional states that overwhelm the person. Positive thoughts result in the dead person experiencing euphoria, while negative thoughts result in feelings of devastation and intense pain. Whatever attitudes and desires the person had in life largely determines the experience the person goes through during this stage.

It is here that the dead person begins to drift from the chance of a higher existence and begins to wander the Bardo of Rebirth, searching for another physical existence into which to be born. Quickly running out of options, the person begins to seek out a family in order to select a new human incarnation.

During this time, the person encounters visions of men and women engaged in the act of sex and quickly becomes drawn to them. The usual instinct will be to rush toward one of the immediate couples, hoping to find a vortex that will lead the person into the womb in order to get away from the confusion of the Bardo world.

The teachings of the Bardo Thodol, an instructional tool for traversing the Bardo states, indicates that the person will be reborn as a man if attracted to the female. If attracted to the male, the person will be born as a woman. The Bardo Thodol describes that it is wise to stay focused and be conscious of not rushing into the first chance at rebirth, as this may lead to a less desirable life. It urges that it is better to remain intent on finding the right family into which to be born in order to gain a chance at a more conscious life in the physical world. This ability to remain aware of choosing the best life into which to be reborn is a technique described as the 'method for closing the womb door' until the most appropriate womb is found.

There are less desirable worlds below the physical one that can be entered if the person does not reincarnate into the material world. These are lower realms that consist of a heaven world, a hell world, a ghost world, a demigod world and an animal world. Such worlds exist to receive good or bad karma, as defined by the previous actions of the person's prior life, and are not conducive to creating new karma that can prepare the person for the next life.

It is somewhat ironic that the heaven world is viewed in Buddhism as an undesirable place to be, for the reason that no significant learning occurs there. The heaven world does not allow for creativity and compassion and is seen more as a holiday resort where little spiritual growth takes place. Like a vacation spot, the person's stay is only temporary. At some point, after their karmic credits have been used up, the person will have to leave and return to the Bardo.

TRANSFORMATION

There is much more to the teachings of the Bardo states than what is briefly described above, although that is the essence of it in as short a span as seems practical. Beyond the Bardo states of the afterlife, there is also the Bardo of Waking Life, The Bardo of Dreaming and the Bardo of Meditating. In the tradition that is the definition of the Bardo meaning, life in the physical world is just as much an in-between place as is the afterlife.

In all, most people spend roughly forty-five days in the afterlife by the time they are in the Bardo of Becoming, with a few days after that occurring in the Bardo of Rebirth. Some people occasionally spend more time in the Bardo world, which leads them eventually into one of the lesser worlds below the physical one.

It is interesting that even though many philosophies and religions view the physical world as one of the lower realms of existence, Tibetan Buddhists see it as the most desirable of the lower worlds in which to come. This is due to their view that the physical world allows for the greatest potential toward spiritual development. If we are trying to ascend into a higher existence and we are already of low moral fiber, this could be viewed as an opportunity to rise to a higher level.

The Bardo states of the afterlife also emphasize the need to be well adjusted in the physical life and to be a good person in order to better navigate the after-death states. If a person is the same in the next life as they were during the previous one, they are dooming themselves to the repetition of physical rebirth. It is through living a worthy life and cultivating good thoughts that there is a better chance of ascending to a higher realm of consciousness.

It would be decades following my formative years as a youngster that I would come across *The Tibetan Book of the Dead*. I then obtained an originally translated copy by W. Y. Evans-Wentz. It reads more like scripture than the many more contemporary books that were written after it, but it does hold the most detail, I think. After reading it, I was struck by a number of descriptions that made me question my experience as a newborn and as a youngster.

When I was still quite young I would have repetitive dreams, wherein I would exist in a void of darkness. Sometimes I could sense another presence, but the world largely remained dark and obscure. It seemed I would wander through it for a long time, feeling I would never get out. Eventually I would, however, and when I saw the first flickers of light, I felt great relief.

After reading *The Tibetan Book of the Dead* and going through its description of the Bardo states, I would come to wonder if those dreams were echoes of my returning to a place wherein I still existed in the space between places that is the afterlife.

Also, quite interestingly, the idea that heaven is not the most desirable place to enter is not unique to Buddhism. Hindus also take the stance that heaven is quite like a vacation spot of idyllic beauty where one stays for as long as the karma they have accumulated through their previous life lasts. After that, they return to another realm of existence where they spend more time in an effort to ascend to the highest realm of all. In the end, we are trying to find our way to that place of pure, absolute consciousness and full enlightenment.

On the subject of Hinduism, it is worth noting that this

belief also supports the thought that there are many worlds of existence. Hinduism, which has been around much longer than Buddhism, advocates the existence of many worlds. Hindus envision the universe consisting of multiple planes of reality. Their Puranic texts imply enough possible worlds and variations of existence that it is difficult to say exactly how many there are. It sees the universe as infinite, with the number of alternate universes and realities being equally infinite.

It is also interesting that Hindu philosophy originated the whole concept of multiple worlds and universes long before the idea crystallized into what theoretical physicists now describe as a multiverse. Perhaps by the time we become entrenched in our physical reality and the continuous cycle of death and rebirth, we have sufficiently forgotten our spiritual inclinations. If our true selves have traveled throughout these multiple dimensions for all time —if we are as infinite as reality itself—there must remain remnants of that knowledge in all of us. At times, it seems just a little too coincidental that the laws of nature, as we now know them in our physical world, eventually lead us closer toward spiritual concepts that are quite similar.

10

The Fragmentation of Human Existence

Buddhists maintain that life is suffering. It is a defining aspect of their philosophy. Even Christians believe that much of our demise is predicated on our fear and greed. Our need for gratification is what leads to our eventual downfall and creates frailty in our character. At its most basic core, human nature is torn between the hunger of desire and the anxiety of what will happen if we lose what we desire. Every action we take, along with the very essence of how we structure our lives, is one effort after another to get what we crave most.

This is not as terrible a thing as it might sound. After all, quite often our wants and desires are aimed at our loved ones. Many of our wants are for our children to have a good education and make a life for themselves and for us to take care of our parents after they become too old to do so for themselves.

At its lowest level, however, those desires center primarily around our lust. It is only when we pursue those cravings above all other consideration that we become lost and have surrendered to our most overwhelming emotions.

Usually, this is where we become lost and tend to wander. Out of misguided pursuits, it becomes inevitable that we should return to this life after death, given yet another chance to correct the folly of that human nature which dwells within.

If we are to believe the concept of the Bardo, it is this very detriment that condemns us to continually return into a life of renewed possibility.

The Christian Bible depicts a time wherein we were all united beings, every one of us understanding each other and equally curious of our own existence. It is fabled that long ago we all spoke a common language. During a time when we were so united, we pricked the skies with a certain audacity, hoping to touch God and find a place for ourselves among the heavens. The Tower of Babel was built in order to reach up to that God in an effort to assert our professed importance. As described in the Book of Genesis, however, this collaborative effort did not go over well with our creator.

In return for such a defiant monument, the tower was destroyed and all those upon the earth were flung far and wide, according to the myth. To ensure we would never again unite in such a defiant act, varying dialects were laid upon us, preventing communication and such collaboration from occurring a second time. The result was that we became strange to one another. Unable to breach the language gap with which we were now faced, we became fragmented people who would become wary of one another; isolated and conflicted.

This is just one legend that has been passed down in order to offer some insight as to why we are so splintered as a people. If nothing else, it can be viewed as an ancient tale that explains our inane penchant to destroy one another. Human nature coddles us while simultaneously attempting to rip us to pieces. It is as if we have been dropped into an interactive game where the rules have been set to thwart every possible effort we may have at succeeding. It sometimes seems a sub-routine has been written into the very code of our DNA, which twists our acceptance of one another so that we feel suspicion, contempt and fear.

If this were truly the case, we would never stand a chance at becoming a more spiritually evolved people. It is from the ooze of humanity that we are offered a chance to rise above it and become better for the effort.

Whether Hindu, Catholic, Buddhist, Muslim or any number of the other religions, every faith essentially believes in a divine presence. It is this overall consciousness that is largely responsible for our existence, while earmarking the great folly of our ways through emotional traps. The question remains, why are we like this? Why is it that if we come from a divine origin have we all had these terrible maladies implanted in our chemical and/or spiritual makeup, sabotaging us from the start?

History has shown human nature to have never evolved from the day we were deposited into this world. If anything, we have only become worse. Never have we experienced a spiritual breakthrough that has swept across the world. We evolve in the sense that our science or our culture becomes more advanced, but as far as spirituality, integrity and simple, human decency is concerned, we are largely non-conformists. It seems we are quite happy to go about our lives, taking what we can for ourselves and turning our back on the larger problems that face us as a global community.

Those of us who have accumulated everything we desire become terrified at the prospect of losing just a portion of what we may have gained throughout our lives. This drives some of us to the point where we are quite happy to kill one another in order to keep those physical trinkets that seem to validate our very existence.

The way our life is engineered in this world sometimes appears impossible. It comes across as so unlikely when one takes time to consider it. We see life grow in so many forms. That a tiny seed, barely the size of a fingernail, can grow into a hundred foot tall maple tree seems truly improbable. Yet, we see such things around us so often we take it for granted. We take it so much for granted we accept it as normal that a seed will grow inside a woman, going through much the same metamorphosis. What is so remarkable is how that growing seed will eventually have a personality. Soon enough, it will breathe and talk and think.

This last aspect is sometimes difficult to understand. From where does that personality come? How is it that we have emotions, thoughts and awareness? From where do such esoteric traits derive? If we have them, does the same hold true for a cat, or even a shrub?

The Fragmentation of Human Existence

Within any religion, life and the soul is largely depicted as something beyond human understanding. To this day, scientists can not decipher simple things we all do (I should not really say they are simple as long as we do not fully understand them), such as transferring images through our eyes and into our brain so they appear as three dimensional objects with depth we can actually perceive. We have come far enough to know certain areas of the brain are responsible for sight, sensation and thought, but we are still far from understanding how it all translates and fits together, let alone what the subconscious is, or why we dream.

For beings so mysterious and beyond our own understanding, it seems primeval that we come into the world in such a horrific way, bursting from the womb while simultaneously existing as a spiritual being. Yet, this is how we go from being detached souls, apparently floating in the ether of limitless possibility until we are given an outlet through which to come into this world.

This posits the reason for why so many religions put much emphasis on reproduction and encouraging it in all their peoples. So many religions are adamant about marriage being that sacred bond between a man and a woman in order that they may couple and bring offspring into the world. It makes perfect sense in a world full of chaos. The reason religion encourages raising children in a family environment is so those souls are at least given a chance to defensively learn about the world while fostering emotions of love. It is a strong family environment that equips us to deal with life's challenges as we mature and move ever closer toward that coupling of our own, wherein the cycle of existence can be repeated.

TRANSFORMATION

This would appear to be the main objective of marriage —the recycling of human souls through a structured method of continually bringing other beings into the world. If we are to think about what religion is, within the context of what marriage encourages, it seems to be supporting something similar to a mass production line. The entire system is quite ingenious when looking at it from such a perspective. While it is ingenious, it is also diabolical, beautiful, insane and wondrous. That very thought seems to sum up the experience of life for so many.

Often, here in the West I hear such proclamations from my fellow man (and woman) that perpetual existence and an eternal soul could not possibly be real. The reasoning is simple. They state there is no proof, or that still no one knows to this day, therefore how could life exist before we are even born.

Ancient cultures have known for millenia that we continually exist in varying states. We may not be able to quantify such things as the human spirit after death, but the reason is obvious. Once dead, we exist in completely different terms. Just as some of us, while we sleep, may dream of acquiring great wealth or expensive cars and boats, once awake it is clear we could never bring them back to our waking reality. Believe me, when I was young I used to try. Those things in our night time wanderings exist on a completely separate level of experience. We can no more bring those things back than we can take with us, upon death, what we have acquired in our physical life. All of them exist in alien forms that are quite departed from one another.

But the proof of higher existence remains. We simply

have to define that proof differently than what we have been taught in the developed West.

The Dalai Lama of Tibet is a prime example.

Having been the country's spiritual leader for hundreds of years, he chooses to reincarnate in our physical world after each death for the sole purpose of guiding others toward enlightenment. For all our self-ordained problems, we could certainly use the help. The very method he employs in finding his way back to physical reality upon each death makes use of the same process after every extinction and every reincarnation.

The inner circle of the Dalai Lama, known as the High Lamas—those who look over their spiritual leader's physical continuation—is tasked with finding the next incarnation of their divine guide following each death. If cremation is the last, physical transformation of the Dalai Lama at his end, the High Lamas follow the direction of the smoke in order to determine the place from where the new incarnation will come. Meditating by central Tibet's sacred lake, Lhamo La-Tso, and seeking visions and signs within dreams, the High Lamas await clues of where to seek out the next embodiment of their sacred oracle.

Always, they search for a young boy who has been born around the same time the last Dalai Lama has died. It usually takes several years before finding the boy, waiting for his cognitive awareness to form adequately enough to be able to pass some rigorous, and secretive, tests. Those tests reveal to the High Lamas whether the boy in question is truly the reincarnated soul of their spiritual leader. Some of these tests are accordingly classified and never revealed to the public, but one of which we do know is that a number of items are placed before the candidate, which the reincarnated Dalai Lama must then select. From a host of objects, the boy must identify the few among them that belonged to him during his previous life. If this is done correctly and the other tests are passed, the candidate has now proved he is the reincarnated form of the Dalai Lama.

That the Dalai Lama can reincarnate without having to spend undue time in the Bardo, where most other peoples' soul is tested, is already fantastic enough on its own. That he is cognitively aware of doing this at his own choosing is reminiscent of those who move through lucid dreams, able to manipulate them to their own will.

It is those final tests the Dalai Lama passes that proves to anyone with memory and faith that awareness exists outside our plane of reality and that we come in and out of it at our own behest. That some have already transcended this reality and elect to return to this world of their own free will is testament to a love they have for all of us. This shows there remains a reason we should be coddled, guided and held dearly as journeying souls bound for greater awareness.

11

The Illusive and the Transparent

The deeper we travel into our own reality and the natural world around us, the more we discover how divine is that which transcends the physical. Our impossible task is to reconcile an existence that lies beyond our known universe. Science lays out a pathway which can be traversed once we know the rules of the road. The problem is, we are seeking something at the end of that road which does not even travel the same way as do we.

What is divinity, after all, but an idea of something that dwells apart from our understanding and remains above our own, mortal awareness. Our fault is attempting to quantify an ideal, which we still have not quite learned to define, into a context that makes sense in the here and now. For as long as we dwell within two—maybe even more than just two—fluctuating states of awareness, from sleep to wake and from death to life, we will rarely glimpse the truth that hides within that thin sliver that separates ourselves from everything else.

Consciousness and New Life

For anyone who believes in reincarnation among those in the developed West, there is a question of when a soul actually attaches itself to a newly growing person.

I began to think about this within the context of my own experience, especially after I wrote Chapter 9. The description I included of the Bardo got me wondering at what stage does the soul actually inhabit the physical body of the developing fetus. Since that was actually the last chapter I wrote—I injected it into the book after having written Remnants—I was curious as to how others may have developed their own physical cognition as they came into being. From what I encountered, my consciousness took form in this world upon birth. I then began to wonder if this was a common occurrence for all.

What I have come to discover after researching the topic is that this can vary, especially from one culture to another. While some peoples believe the soul enters the form of a new human being at conception, or sometimes not long following it, others believe this does not happen until the actual birth, and sometimes even shortly after birth. There is also a belief that some souls hover around a woman before she has actually conceived.

In some parts of the world, where the belief in reincarnation has existed for a very long time indeed, it is said that a soul will often jump in and out of a growing baby, sometimes hovering around the newly forming fetus while deciding if this is the body it wishes to inhabit. If that soul eventually chooses to move on, another will quickly move in and take its place.

It is not uncommon for the pregnant woman to have a dream involving the child before it is even born. This is said to be due to the psychic connection the soul establishes with the mother-to-be as it inhabits the fetus and goes about forming the development of its psyche. There is also a belief that the holographic projection of the soul helps to shape the form the newly born person will take following birth and as they grow.

While some of this may remain a cultural interpretation, it seems quite dependent on the individual soul regardless of culture. Much of it may revolve around how aware that consciousness may be and whether it enters life blindly, or purposely chooses a gross body to suit its own needs. The latter may be the reason for child prodigies who appear to take few traits from their parents while impressing a surprising knowledge on the rest of the world as they mature.

All forms of this type of belief is not taken by such cultures as something that is either true or false. Instead, it is emphatically accepted that this is how the process takes place, no matter of the above mentioned nuances.

Endless Souls

Because the developed world places much faith in empirical measurement and finite concepts, those of us here in the West often question the validity of reincarnation when we see how quickly the earth's population is growing. After all, how can souls simply reincarnate while people continue to become more abundant?

This is perhaps where we are better served to open our minds to concepts of infinity.

Hinduism has long espoused a limitless universe that grows and expands while other universes around it do the same. Much of theoretical physics follows a similar train of thought. Universes and other worlds are created constantly within this belief system. While some worlds eventually approach their end, others are being born. If we do move between different realities, it could be that those worlds, which are harbored in all those endless universes, are taking us in and then watching us leave from one to the next.

There is also the Buddhist belief that there are many other realms where consciousness dwells, not the least of which are the lower ones. At some point, when the conscious souls from those other realms have evolved to the point of leaving, it would be practical to think that some of them are going to end up within our own reality. If true existence is limitless and constantly being created, there would naturally be an influx at one point or another, not the least of which would be this world.

We should also look at the concept that consciousness has often been touted in some old philosophies as being slivers that are derived from a larger whole. Each sliver is, in fact, the very same consciousness. This overall cognizance—what some may describe as a Supreme Being —would also be without limit. Concepts of existence could therefore be as limitless as imagination itself.

Veil

Anyone who has been alive and dead, floating even just momentarily between those two places, has the chance to know within that instant the truth of reality. This is the place between space. There is a moment wherein we all transfer from one realization into another. For a brief moment, both places appear to be real. In truth, both *are* real. As real as we know, that is.

Life and death are as equally real and equally illusive. Reality is a state of consciousness. We perceive something to be real, therefore it is. We can be in one place and know beyond a shadow of a doubt that it exists. As far as we know, life in this world is as real as it gets. Yet, for anyone who has transitioned just briefly into another reality, this life is suddenly not so convincing. Existence becomes momentarily detached. Those who have briefly died soon see this world as quite less than substantial. They see it that way until they gradually forget the world they saw behind the curtain.

Repetition has a way of convincing the susceptible mind.

Those who are devout in their affirmation that the existence beyond sight remains a state of pure consciousness carry that knowledge with them into the next world they choose to inhabit. There, we remain suspended long enough to see ourselves while infinity unfolds before us. Then we are transformed once more. We have moved on from one place into the next. There we will dwell...for a while. Then, at some point, we will blink. After that, nothing else is ever the same.

12

Remnants

The Minutia of Separation

We know our nature plainly enough. Many of us, even if we are not aware of it, feel it as part of our very being. It is the scourge that causes our hatred and rebellion, lashing out at the very meaning of existence.

This is not our world. Our anger is deep seeded and many of us do not know why. The very essence of that contempt lies buried within the darkest reaches of our memories. The land in which we exist is a mirage that taunts us and constantly whispers we are fools for not seeing the truth throughout our lives. It is that part of us which feels all too clearly what we choose to deny in order to survive this place. Deep down, however, we know what it is that hides from view. It flickers past our awareness every time we close our eyes and take a deep breath. The illusion is real, just as every other illusion so painfully is.

The vast majority of human integrity and its lack thereof lies in one simple truth. So buried in our mind, disguised as part of our intellect, is the knowledge that the life we lead is obscured behind something else. It is that part of our subconscious that urges us to tear the world apart just so we can see what is hidden beneath.

We are beings who have been thrust into this life, flawed and realizing from birth that this place is not worthy of us. So, we do what any adolescent does when angered and feeling betrayed. We lash out and destroy everything we feel matters to us, along with our brothers, sisters and neighbors. By destroying the world, we hope it will reveal itself as the illusion we have so long suspected. We may fear to say as much, but we know it nevertheless. It is why we hold our own fears and doubts close to our chest while wondering if our next door neighbor is feeling the same.

None of us would ever admit as much to one another, so we do the next best thing. We impress our doubts and fears on our fellow humans, hoping they will be the first to crack and show the truth that lies within. When they fail to do so, we destroy their world, along with ours, hoping that something will finally split apart in the process. The problem is no one wants to take that first step as long as there is the possibility of being revealed as the fool.

Genius and singular thinking is not the domain of the popular mindset.

Perhaps it is within this sliver of understanding that human nature resides, reluctant to show itself as something grander than what we have already glimpsed. We all have flickers of brilliance but too many of us seem incapable of translating them. As soon as they are seen, they are as quickly burned up and cast aside for practicality's sake. Better to move along with the herd, for the good of us all.

Our essence is beyond what we can hope to glean in one, brief lifetime. This is why we live with the nagging tug of a reminder that tells us we are all waiting for something more. Physical reality is as false as the processed flavors sprinkled on our local fast food delight and keeps us coming back for more. For that reason, we are happy to accept those falsehoods for a passing moment of self-indulgence, no matter the empty calories.

Existence remains an imitation of our own mind and its conscious projections. No wonder the truly myopic—the madmen of our time—have built empires for our appeasement. The nearest horizon beyond our immediate sight is simply too frightening to consider. Behind the veils with which we choose to shroud ourselves, we continue to know there is something more pertinent than what we choose to see. It lingers just out of sight, far enough away that we rarely have to face it. We know one day it will all come falling down. When it does, we will be there standing on the threshold of life and death, either ready to confront it or eager to simply turn away again, too blinded by what we have conditioned ourselves to believe every waking moment until then.

The Grand Design

It may be safe to say that life is not so much about every one of our singular needs as it is about something we must achieve along the way. When we see this clearly, existence takes on new meaning. The world is no longer what we expect. Our lives here, as separate as they may have been in the past, become transformed.

The world, as we have previously seen it, becomes moot. We move past those barriers that have kept us down and unable to rise to a higher level of awareness.

This is our legacy. It remains every person's opportunity to move beyond their own limits and to cast off material concerns in order to become larger than life, once again moving in a single direction.

Look past petty greed and embrace selfless purpose. The world will see this and reverberate. Everything in this reality is temporary, after all. It is best to be grateful for what it has chosen to show.

While many spiritual philosophies, as diverse as they may be throughout the world, are suggesting they share a common theme, we so often miss the point they strive to impart. While subtly reminding us that religion and belief is markedly similar from one culture to another, we seem determined to use skewed interpretations as an excuse to keep each other at a distance. It is all quite contrary to the deeper meaning that implores us to go to one another; to be familiar and deserving of each other.

It could be that none of us are really here to become a greater civilization than what we already are. Human races, which have come before us only to be incinerated in an irrecoverable ash, seem to clearly demonstrate that one civilization does not pass on its lessons to the next. We are simply biding time as we dance about and indulge our baser instincts while sinking toward self-destruction like so many worlds and cultures before us.

Still, none of it is without meaning. After all, if it were

meaningless why would new civilizations pop up following thousands of years of previously failed experiments? Could it be we come back to frolic in a world unlike our own ethereal existence, where the misdeeds in which we partake are never as serious or lasting as what it seems to us here. Maybe our lot is nothing more than to experience an existence that is fated from the start to burn itself out? It is not so requisite that we create something better, but perhaps it is more important we build something we can then destroy, for no other reason than to learn from its annihilation.

In the end, there remain those who do their best to elevate the rest of us beyond our physical binds in order to prompt us to excel past moments of wasted indulgence. It remains a struggle against forsaken awareness.

Great civilizations such as the Sumerians of Mesopotamia, ancient Greeks and Egyptians—even the British Empire and the United States (granted, the end result of the last mentioned still remains to be seen)— never managed to change the world in a spiritually awakened way. They may have elevated their intellect during those brief moments, but their empires eventually all collapsed. It would be ostentatious to think we could do what no one else has ever done in any existence before ours. All we can hope is to learn the same things those before us learned and to carry them into the next world, knowing that everything we did, here in this life, made us better for the effort.

Despite the waste we leave behind, there is always something more that comes out of us. Everyone does what they may in order to individually discover that hidden treasure for which most of us subconsciously search.

Remnants

Many of us may never know what this world is and what it truly means—at least not while we are in it—but we can take a piece of its good qualities and infuse it within ourselves. After all, any of its better properties are a result of our own doing.

The world beyond physical sight requires a higher awareness. Some of us do perceive another reality that awaits the more cultivated mind. It is a remnant that reminds us we are never more than partially here.

If there is one thing enabling us to cut through that shroud, it is the realization that everything around us has been constructed to enrapture us. Superficial trinkets can be swept aside by one simple realization. All of us share the same reality and sense of being, regardless of race or religion. This is easily confirmed by the simple fact that we all suffer from the same human flaws. We are controlled by the same emotions that stem from our fear and greed, no matter what our belief system may be and no matter what our culture teaches. Whatever our upbringing, we are plagued by examples of wandering off the path to enlightenment, simply by suffering the temptations of life. We lust, we greed, we fear and we doubt. We doubt ourselves and all those before us who strive to teach, while too often remaining the same.

As a youngster, I grew up believing we were here to make the world a better place and to end suffering everywhere. As years dragged on, it seemed fewer people were concerned with such pursuits. It appeared as if much of the world was simply not interested.

It then became clear, along with the meaning. The eternal question that many seem ill equipped to answer has nothing to do with some fleeting notion that is lost to obscurity due to esoteric nuances beyond comprehension. The purpose of life is no more mysterious than to simply exist and to journey as far as our insight will allow. We are all here to experience something physical. Whether that means lofty pleasures or exquisite torments, such experiences are almost inseparable. We can help others along the way or destroy them, but in the end it is all the same. Every act is there to enrich us, whether or not we are the orchestrator of that act.

It may seem an abstract notion, but if we really stop to think about the concept it soon becomes obvious. After all, we would have to be very impressive beings to bring about such grandiose changes as a new world order; something which has not yet happened throughout the eons we have existed.

We remain mystical beings, brimming with restrained energy. Hidden within us is such will that we are able to transform ourselves in order to occupy the physical world where we are free to travel the playgrounds of our creation. Life in this world is as much a dream in the sense that it only exists at the behest of our own designs. We may not remember that simple truth, but it remains so that we can experience it to its fullest. After all, it is we who have placed ourselves into this world, intentionally or otherwise. In that sense we are all travelers of life, searching for that path that eventually leads us back to the place from where we come.

Conclusion

It often seems beyond belief that reality could possibly be a distorted interpretation of what we believe to be real at any given moment. We are so fully enveloped in the world that nothing else which dares to challenge our current notions could possibly be real. Yet, this is the great barrier that separates us from what we know, in our hearts, and what we come to accept as singular awakening.

Through these pages, I have offered thoughts that will challenge some peoples' idea of what is reality. There will be some who will simply scoff at these notions and declare them preposterous. Yet, thousands of years of evidence has built a solid mass that has defied contemporary beliefs and lent credence to the propositions I have put forth.

Our existence in this world is a flicker that equates to little more than a prolonged dream. I keeps us as dizzy and disoriented as any other dream we have throughout this brief life. That a dream could be anything more than a delirious afterthought seems beyond reckoning. Yet, dreams transport us from one conscious state of being into another, while simultaneously destroying the barriers that keep us separated from such far-flung ideas in the first place.

The great denominator is consciousness.

Those who practice ancient philosophies here in the West, hoping to find that elusive secret they have heard so much about, are sometimes not quite sure what they seek. Those who feel close to that higher plane practice the latest fads, whether they be yoga, tantric sex or meditation, hoping to discover what our own lives have failed to do so far. Yet, if we practice them while fully aware, they offer higher insight.

Such pursuits, for many of us, seem a wasted effort. What is yoga, after all? What are we hoping to achieve? Is it just the latest craze—a recycled one, at that—or is it something developed by a very old culture with which we have little in common?

For many of us, yoga is a way to hone our bodies. Beyond that, however, it is something far more spiritual than some of us will know. Even meditation seems a freaky notion with which we are not fully conversant. Meditation helps us calm our mind and put the latest day's dilemmas to rest, but that is a far cry from what it offers in potential.

Some who pursue such practices are possibly not clear on exactly where it might take them. Meditation, if performed correctly, breaks down the walls of illusion and catapults us into a reality beyond that which some may be prepared to see. This is the doorway beyond physical reality; the one which leads into death and awakens the awe that is pure existence. As much as some of us fear our deeper dreams and what they may mean, we are likely less ready for the doors of perception to open and offer a glimpse into the alternate reality that is our existence beyond death.

Once we come to see our life as far more than a fleeting indulgence, reality and our own take on it comes into focus. We are nothing less than enigmatic travelers set on a course with no immediately clear path other than to discover true clarity. For many of us, that moment will remain elusive as we carry out our orchestrated acts to our perceived good. Existence holds us fast but the truth of our very essence offers its hand while proposing a way toward brighter ends.

There is no mystery other than the one we create for ourselves. For so long, time has offered a simple explanation. Pay attention and the decree toward illumination will be unleashed. The answer continues to shine before us, eventually smiling without reserve as it sees that brilliant recognition in our eyes. Soon enough we receive that opportunity to see it clearly.

Altered Perceptions

Just as much as reality is perceived, so is time. Even perception exists only in the way we interpret it. As much as we may come to accept our physical life as an altered form of reality, the same holds true for time.

What is time, after all, other than an abstract notion to which we pay a certain amount of homage. It is as much a product of our projected mind as the rest of our physical reality. Time dwells within a finite realm that struggles to bring order out of disorder. The walls of our own physical reality come closer into view the more we impose finite order to infinite chaos.

Does time really exist in the way we have taught ourselves to believe?

An idea that challenges this notion is to say that, yes, there is a finite world that is governed by constrictions of time, but if we were to suppose our universe has multiple levels and that time only exists within its 3-dimensional construct, the finite world would lose its meaning. Step outside that infinite universe and suddenly all notions of physical reality dissolve.

How could such a thing be possible? If the universe is infinite, how could we possibly step outside its barriers? The logical supposition is that there are no barriers if it is truly without end. If there is no end, how could we step beyond this reality and all the impressions we have fabricated around it?

This is where we have to think in differing terms to what we have become accustomed. Infinity does not reside solely within the macro dynamics of our reality. There remains that region beyond physical space. If the universe is truly endless we may still have the ability to step outside it simply by moving past its dimensional imperatives for the sake of those not yet seen from our own perspective. Eternity continues within the inter-dimensional, as well as the outer spheres of our known reality. Time is a moment in existence, but that existence continues beyond physical limitation.

This idea transfers to all perceptions of reality, as it does constrictions of space-time. It would be decades before I eventually saw that the 'block universe theory' (See

Appendix, A New Model of Time) actually substantiated those intuitive senses I carried that seemed to conflict with learned notions of time.

The premise of the block universe theory (which derives its basis from Einstein's work on relativity) suggests our perception of time only exists within our known universe. Beyond our universe, it has been theorized that time may not exist at all. Outside 4-dimensional space-time we begin to confront higher dimensional realms where the extent of our knowledge gets thrown out the window.

The strange thing is that if time does exist in the way we imagine, even then it only exists the way we perceive it within our spatial reality of three dimensions. For all those dimensions beyond the ones in which we currently find ourselves, our idea of time would be completely different; perhaps even nonexistent. Time may still exist, but in forms we can not quite grasp while existing within a physical reality.

What is more intriguing than even that is how our consciousness interprets further dimensions and realities. Because our consciousness is always flitting in and out of altered realities, thoughts of time could be prone to dissolving and losing their meaning. This is how we are able to see beyond our interpretations of the physical world. Some of us are actually able to retain memories of time, or its lack thereof, during each instance our awareness comes back to 3-dimensional reality. Hence the reason for some of us to circumvent such restrictions and see future events that have already happened.

This is the realm of alternate realities where death disappears and existence takes on new meaning. All reality happens at once, beyond time and space. How we break past those barriers that keep us grounded within a 3-dimensional world is the true realization.

During a simple dream, time dissipates. Dreaming truly is a transformation of consciousness, which destroys all sense of time, whether some of us understand this or not. It reminds us that for as long as we live we always have one foot in this world and one foot out.

If we see in this world that we truly are connected to everything else, we are awake. I experienced this knowledge deeply during an off-hand, rainy day during a break from school. This is what has been described as cosmic consciousness. It is the thing that remains in our core after everything else has fallen away.

Wisdom of the Ancients

More cultures exist on the planet who believe in a soul, or spirit, which carries on long after death than those who do not. Much of this asserting comes from years of practice and developed awareness.

There still exists, to this day, a huge divide between the Far East and the newly developed West. We young prodigies of the New World find ourselves in a privileged condition, evolving through our technological achievements in so short an order.

But herein lies the problem. We do remain a new civilization. Perhaps we have grown too fast, thus losing the intuition of our ancestors. Patience is pushed toward the background in order that we are able to satisfy our newly found appetite. We are too busy chasing our aspirations. It may be more common for a burgeoning culture to catapult itself far beyond average ability than previously thought. There is clear evidence and examples of similar leaps and bounds which have occurred in the past. This phenomenon seems to be a recurring order, which perhaps changes us for a reason; hopefully for the better.

Here, in our pocket of the world, many of us discount eternal consciousness. As a result, some have turned their back on spirituality and have embraced something of which they can clearly make sense. History and folklore are ripe with civilizations that have done the same. Usually, the story of such pursuit ends with extinction. Throughout those times, the oldest cultures among us succeed in carrying on in spite of that brief audacity.

It is only in our mind that proof of eternal existence is fleeting. Our much older brethren have seen evidence of it throughout ages. Their affirmation comes by means we in the West still do not fully appreciate. More enlightened beings return to the land east of us, where retained memories are in greater abundance, than they do here. For those who have traversed the place between death and birth and have chosen to return to our world, the gift for such sacrifice is greater awareness while here in the land of the living. Such cultures revisit their higher plane through means that are simply too time consuming and disciplined for our technological world to tolerate. What proof we wish to satisfy our own curiosity is expected in a timely manner so we do not waste seconds and minutes we could otherwise be spending on more productive pursuits.

Older cultures have been to places we only imagine, returning with the proof clinging to them. Quite often, if such cultures wish to visit their ancestral grounds, which lie beyond the physical plane of our knowledge, they are free to do so through means that still escape our understanding. That some of us can unlock our consciousness and travel to realms beyond static understanding seems too abstract a notion for many to accept as real within our own definition of reality.

For those wise ancients, the question is not a matter of *if* existence continues beyond life; it is more a question of what form it might take.

What our ancestors have known for thousands of years is simple, yet eagerly denied. Consciousness flits without end. Throughout our life, each of us moves in and out of, and between, every waking moment we interpret as real. Science has been unable to deny as much, but masks such realizations as commonplace by merely interpreting those fluctuations as mental discrepancies the 'experts' are still attempting to decode. Every hallucination we experience when not getting enough sleep, along with every bump on the head that causes our mind to momentarily wander, as well as every Near Death Experience and dream state, is a reverberation that sends our consciousness into another world of experience where every reality is interpreted by our current state of mind. That, along with the levels of awakening to which we travel, dictate what is real at any given moment. For as long as that is the truth, brain, mind and consciousness remain far departed ideas that maintain their own domain.

From all those concepts that have been actualized by simply examining the evidence, death should be recognized as the least of our concerns. It remains a moment in the span of eternity. Some of us encounter instances that seem beyond physical reason. We exist within an infinite expanse, constantly moving in and out of varying conditions of perception and conscious states of reality. Those events that seem to deny our physical existence and bring our acceptance of what is real into question is nothing less than an echo among the halls of memory as we move into one reality for the sake of another.

We may experience events that seem paranormal, but that is only to be taken within the context of our current existence. Inside eternal consciousness dwells the awakening mind. Until we are fully awake, each moment remains a riddle waiting to be deciphered.

Appendix

A New Model of Time

After I finished writing *Transformation*, certain topics I had described continued to linger in my mind. One of the subjects with which I grappled most was that of time. Existence was easy. I, like everyone else, simply move in and out of one reality and another. Time, however, was something that continued to cling to me in this life like a tacky aversion.

Just as existence was simple, so was eternity. All seemed so clear and easy to understand before this singular life.

It is the two forces of contradiction that continued to pull at me. Eternity pushes against time. One has no end, whereas the other insists upon it in order to make sense of ourselves in this world. Time cements us within our physical reality in order that we are able to cope. Without time we are free to wander beyond limit. If we were to bring such knowledge into this world it would be a great burden as we become inundated with counting the minutes of our life, until finally (gratefully!) moving past it.

After completing the thoughts I felt compelled to put in the form of written word, I kept going back to it. Could time really never exist, just as I always believed? I had to wonder. It seemed obvious enough, even after being born.

There *was* no time. Everything was all at once.

Physical existence puts its spell on us, though I continued to research the subject, seeking order out of disorder. That is how I eventually stumbled upon the 'block universe theory'. After that, everything I had suspected suddenly made sense.

I was not crazy after all. There were others who believed in time the same way as did I. Einstein was the great prognosticator. He took a notion many of us undoubtedly sense and turned it into qualified science.

This is how it works...

Imagine the universe as a block—a chunk—of space-time. As Einstein demonstrated, space and time exist within the same construct. How we interpret that space and time depends on our perspective from within the same vantage point. Many of us will rarely know, however, what lies beyond that chunk of space-time. As far as a number of us believe, there is nothing else outside our known universe.

Now let us penetrate the barriers of that 4-dimensional space-time.

If we were to step outside our familiar universe, we could look back at it and see space as it exists within a 3-dimensional context. Because we are able to see it all at once, we can also see the forth dimension that is part of that same space. Therefore, time would exist all at once. We would be able to see it from high upon our precipice, just as we would be able to see all space at once. If we saw just one person within that space, who happened to be eating their supper at one point within the block universe, we would also be able to see their life a bit further on in that same space and time, wherein they are eventually hit by a bus while crossing the street. That person would not be able to see their own future, but we would be able to see all moments at once while standing outside physical space-time.

It is a fairly provocative and tingly idea. Some may deny this possibility. Then there are others who state it is more than likely, not just due to their philosophical inclinations, but also because science has laid out a plausible trail that can actually lead to this end.

Given these ideas, it becomes possible to see how foresight and precognition could make sense within a scientific dynamic.

What is particularly fascinating about time existing in this way inside a block universe is that I already had this intuition even before stumbling upon it. There was always a part of me that simply was not convinced of the traditional concept of what many of us consider to be time.

It makes sense that time should be distorted into the form it takes while we are alive in this world. Physical life is finite and it makes sense to us. Time follows a linear path, as far as we are aware, because it works for our current existence. In this place, time must become as much an illusion as the rest of our existence. After all, think how difficult it would be to cope with our physical lives if we saw and experienced existence without time following an ordered sequence. We would realize everything all at once. Everything would be that moment of 'now'. We would be as aware of the future as well as the past and we would exist in all of them at once. As pure consciousness, that may be possible. It seems very unlikely that anyone could exist a lifetime in this world while experiencing no ordered sequence to events. That reality would simply be too alien for us to exist without so much undue insanity tearing at what we have come to accept as real. As long as we pursue a physical existence, it is in our interest to follow the ordered rules of the natural world.

Australian Aborigine Spiritualism

The Aborigines of Australia have a fairly particular belief in their spiritual essence. The philosophy of their reality is very much a form of animism, though they have specifically defined it through their own beliefs.

There are things about their beginning that stem from a time before their incarnation within the physical world. This is what they refer to as the Creation Period. The Creation Period is when it was said that the Ancestral Beings formed the physical world. Existing as eternal spirits, the Ancestral Beings took physical form and walked the earth, creating the hills, the woods, the water and all other natural formations. They created human beings, which the souls from the Creation Period inhabited. Upon death, those souls would enter the Dreamtime, wherein they would return to the 'sky-people', where the Ancestral Beings who created them would dwell. There they would exist until being born into another physical form, whether it be human, plant or animal.

The Aborigine belief is that the soul remains eternal. Life within the physical world begins and ends, but the soul continues forever while it lives and dies through the many cycles of death and rebirth. While in the Dreamtime, space and time become disconnected from what we know within the physical world. Space and time are infinite and the distinction between past and present dissolves upon death. The soul is able to reconnect with its ancestors and loved ones and all is known once more, as it was before coming into the physical world.

To Australian Aborigines, the Dreamtime is the natural condition of human consciousness, wherein death is just another cycle as the soul moves through eternity, never ending. Even while asleep, the Dreamtime can be entered, during which the soul leaves the body and can reconnect with its ancestors and loved ones. This belief precedes many of the much younger philosophies and faiths that have been around for only the past several thousand years, but which espouse similar beliefs to this day.

As much as animism can be considered the precursor of all known faiths and philosophies, it also appears to be the most pure and devoid of malicious overtures. Today there are hundreds of different groups of Aboriginal people in Australia—what are referred to as nations—all of whom hold the same belief system, but with varying slants. There may have been many tribes across the planet in the distant past prior to the last 50 to 70 thousand years of Aboriginal existence, of whom we are unaware, but the indigenous people of Australia are clearly the oldest, still living. From what we have discerned, they continue to embrace the same faith we believe was adhered to by the earliest of modern humans.

Time Dating Estimates

It should be pointed out that when I first began writing Transformation, estimates for the length of time the Australian Aborigines and Native North Americans have existed as a continuous culture have subsequently increased. For example, estimates for Australian natives averaged around the 50,000 year mark in 2012/2013. Some current estimates are now guessing the Aborigines as having existed for about 65,000 years. Native North Americans were thought to have inhabited the land for roughly 10,000 years in 2013, whereas they are now believed to have existed continuously for 12,000 to 15,000 years.

Estimates appear to increase over the years as more archeological work is conducted. This guesswork is usually based on such things as carbon dating artifacts and ruins found to have been the product of such cultures.

Bibliography
(and Suggested Reading)

Adhikari, Saugat. "10 oldest Ancient civilizations ever existed." *Ancient History List*. 11 September 2014. 11 October 2016 <https://www.ancienthistorylists.com/ancient-civilizations/10-oldest-ancient-civilizations-ever-existed/>.

"Animism." *Religion Facts*. 28 October 2016. 13 September 2018 <http://www.religionfacts.com/animism>.

Barker, Steven A. "N, N-Dimethyltryptamine (DMT), an Endogenous Hallucinogen: Past, Present, and Future Research to Determine Its Role and Function." *frontiers in Neuroscience*. 6 August 2018. 31 October 2018 <https://www.frontiersin.org/articles/10.3389/fnins.2018.00536/full>.

Burkeman, Oliver. "Why can't the world's greatest minds solve the mystery of consciousness?" *The Guardian*. 21 January 2015. 9 December 2016 <https://www.theguardian.com/science/2015/jan/21/-sp-why-cant-worlds-greatest-minds-solve-mystery-consciousness>.

Bibliography

Carman, Elizabeth. "Soul Enters the Womb." *Ayurmater.* 4
September 2012. 16 December 2017
<http://ayurmater.blogspot.com/2012/09/soul-enters-womb.html>.

Castaneda, Carlos. *A Separate Reality.* New York: Pocket Books.
1971

China Internet Information Center. "Formation of the Chinese
Civilization." Homepage. 2001. 14 December 2016
<http://www.china.org.cn/e-gudai/index-1.htm>.

Clarke, Jerome. "Jacques Vallee Discusses UFO Control System."
UFO Evidence. 1978. 9 September 2018
<http://www.ufoevidence.org/documents/doc608.htm>.

"Australian Aboriginal Dreamtime." *Crystalinks.* 17 November
2017 <http://www.crystalinks.com/dreamtime.html>.

Darin, Paul. "Enduring Mystery Surrounds the Ancient Site of
Puma Punku." *Ancient Origins.* 8 February 2016. 18 October 2018
<https://www.ancient-origins.net/ancient-places-
americas/enduring-mystery-surrounds-ancient-site-puma-punku-
005317>.

Das, Subhamoy. "What You Need to Know About the Vedas—
India's Most Sacred Texts." *ThoughtCo.* 3 May 2018. 5 September
2018 <https://www.thoughtco.com/what-are-vedas-1769572>.

Davis, Kathleen. "Everything you need to know about DMT."
Medical News Today. 24 March 2017. 29 October 2018
<https://www.medicalnewstoday.com/articles/306889.php>.

DerSarkissian, Carol. "Facts About Dreaming." *WebMD.* 17
September 2016. 21 December 2017
<https://www.webmd.com/sleep-disorders/guide/dreaming-
overview#1>.

Easwaran, Eknath. *The Bhagavad Gita*. Tomales: Nilgiri Press. 2007

Evans-Wentz, W. Y. *The Tibetan Book of The Dead*. New York: Oxford University Press. 2000

Faulkner, Raymond O. *Ancient Egyptian Book of the Dead*. New York: Barnes and Noble. 2011

Folger, Tim. "If an Electron Can Be in Two Places at Once, Why Can't You?" *Discover Magazine*. 5 June 2005. 11 November 2017 <http://discovermagazine.com/2005/jun/cover>.

Fox, Maggie. "Fewer Americans Believe in God—Yet They Still Believe in Afterlife." *NBC News*. 21 March 2016. 5 October 2017 <https://www.nbcnews.com/better/wellness/fewer-americans-believe-god-yet-they-still-believe-afterlife-n542966>.

Goldhill, Olivia. "Science can't totally explain consciousness, and it never will." *Quartz*. 19 June 2016. 22 December 2017 <https://qz.com/708632/science-cant-totally-explain-consciousness-and-it-never-will/>.

Grady, Denise. "The Vision Thing: Mainly in the Brain." *Discover Magazine*. 1 June 1993. 6 September 2018 <http://discovermagazine.com/1993/jun/thevisionthingma227>.

Greg, TD. "Jacques Vallee – On Messengers of Deception." *Daily Grail*. 17 July 2008. 5 March 2017 <https://www.dailygrail.com/2008/07/jacques-vallee-on-messengers-of-deception/>.

Greene, Brian. *The Hidden Reality*. New York: Vintage Books. 2011

Griffin, Andrew. "Project Star Gate: CIA Makes Details of its

Bibliography

Psychic Control Plans Public." *Independent*. 18 January 2017. 1
September 2018 <https://www.independent.co.uk/life-
style/gadgets-and-tech/news/project-star-gate-cia-central-
intelligence-agency-a7534191.html>.

Hamer, Ashley. "Believe It or Not, Science Still Can't Explain
Gravity." *Curiosity*. 17 July 2017. 5 January 2018
<https://curiosity.com/topics/believe-it-or-not-science-still-cant-
explain-gravity-curiosity/>.

Hawking, Stephen. *A Brief History of Time*. London: Transworld
Publishers. 2008

Hein, Simeon. "Do We Live in a Holographic Universe?" *Gaia*. 1
June 2017. 27 August 2017 <https://www.gaia.com/lp/content/do-
we-live-in-a-holographic-universe-simeon-hein/>.

Howell, Elizabeth. "Parallel Universes: Theories & Evidence."
Space. 9 May 2018. 3 September 2018
<https://www.space.com/32728-parallel-universes.html>.

Keel, John A. *The Mothman Prophecies*. New York: Tor Books.
2002

Kramer, Melody. "The Physics Behind Schrodinger's Cat
Paradox." *National Geographic*. 14 August 2013. 31 August 2018
<https://news.nationalgeographic.com/news/2013/08/130812-
physics-schrodinger-erwin-google-doodle-cat-paradox-science/>.

Laliberte, Marissa. "10 Ancient Mysteries Researchers Still Can't
Explain." *Reader's Digest*. 2018. 13 September 2018
<https://www.rd.com/culture/ancient-mysteries/>.

Lin, Tao. "DMT: You Cannot Imagine a Stranger Drug or a
Stranger Experience." *Vice*. 5 August 2014. 22 January 2017
<https://www.vice.com/en_ca/article/5gkkpd/dmt-you-cannot-

imagine-a-stranger-drug-or-a-stranger-experience-365>.

MacDonald, Fiona. "Reality Doesn't Exist Until We Measure It, Quantum Experiment Confirms." *Science Alert*. 1 June 2015. 20 October 2017 <https://www.sciencealert.com/reality-doesn-t-exist-until-we-measure-it-quantum-experiment-confirms>.

Mark, Joshua. "Osiris." *Ancient History Encyclopedia*. 6 March 2016. 9 September 2018 <https://www.ancient.eu/osiris/>.

Mark, Joshua. "The Afterlife in Ancient Greece." *Ancient History Encyclopedia*. 18 January 2012. 10 September 2018 <https://www.ancient.eu/article/29/the-after-life-in-ancient-greece/>.

Martin, Sean. "Time is NOT real: Physicists show EVERYTHING happens at the same time." *Express*. 3 December 2016. 7 January 2018 <https://www.express.co.uk/news/science/738387/Time-NOT-real-EVERYTHING-happens-same-time-einstein>.

Morse, Melvin. "NDE Required to Rule Ancient Egypt?" *Spiritual Scientific*. 10 June 2010. 8 August 2018 <http://spiritualscientific.com/DrMorseBlog/2010/06/10/nde-required-to-rule-ancient-egypt/>.

Nichols, Hannah. "Dreams: Why do we dream?" *Medical News Today*. 28 June 2018. 2 September 2018 <https://www.medicalnewstoday.com/articles/284378.php>.

Oldale, Richard. "14 Mysterious Lokas of Hindu Mythology Explained." *Antaryami*. 11 December 2017. 7 July 2017 <https://www.antaryami.com/hinduism/mysterious-14-lokas-hindu-mythology/>.

Osho. *Book of Secrets: 112 Meditations to Discover the Mystery Within*. New York: St. Martin's Press. 2010

Bibliography

Parry, Emma. "Airmen involved in 'British Roswell' may have been abducted by aliens, retired US colonel claims in secret footage." *The Sun*. 15 January 2018. 2 April 2018 <https://www.thesun.co.uk/news/5331467/airmen-involved-in-british-roswell-incident-may-have-been-abducted-by-aliens-retired-us-colonel-reveals-in-secret-footage/>.

Poirier, Bill. "Quantum Weirdness and Many Interacting Worlds." *The Huffington Post*. 12 November 2014. 20 January 2017 <https://www.huffingtonpost.com/bill-poirier/quantum-weirdness-and-many-interacting-worlds_b_6143042.html>.

Puzzo, Alberto. "A Quantum Delayed-Choice Experiment." *Science*. 338 November 2012: 634-637.

Reneke, Dave. "NASA Research To Create A 'Warp Drive' Bubble In Lab." *Dave Reneke's World of Space and Astronomy*. 23 May 2016. 22 September 2018 <https://www.davidreneke.com/nasa-research-to-create-a-warp-drive-bubble-in-lab/>.

Shimojo, Shinsuke. "What visual perception tells us about mind and brain." *PNAS*. 23 October 2001. 5 September 2018 <http://www.pnas.org/content/98/22/12340>.

Sloat, Sarah. "Why Can't We Hear Our Hearts Beat? Here's How Our Brain Turns Down the Volume." *Huffington Post*. 6 December 2017. 8 March 2018 <https://www.huffingtonpost.com/inverse/why-cant-we-hear-our-hear_b_9909322.html>.

Stephen, Juan. "What are the most widely practiced religions of the world?" *The Register*. 6 October 2006. 6 January 2016 <https://www.theregister.co.uk/2006/10/06/the_odd_body_religion/>.

Strassman, Rick. *DMT: The Spirit Molecule*. Rochester: Park Street Press. 2000

Susskind, Leonard. *The Black Hole War.* New York: Little, Brown and Company. 2008

Taylor, Steve. "Cosmic Consciousness." *Psychology Today.* 13 March 2017. 2 November 2017 <https://www.psychologytoday.com/ca/blog/out-the-darkness/201703/cosmic-consciousness>.

The Dalai Lama. "Reincarnation." *His Holiness the 14th Dalai Lama of Tibet.* 24 September 2011. 3 November 2016 <https://www.dalailama.com/messages/retirement-and-reincarnation/reincarnation>.

Vallee, Jacques. *Confrontations: A Scientist's Search for Alien Contact.* New York: Ballantine Books. 1990

Vikoulov, Alex. "From the Holographic Principle to the Holofractal Principle." *Ecstadelic.* 15 May 2017. 14 August 2017 <https://www.ecstadelic.net/ecstadelic/from-the-holographic-principle-to-the-holofractal-principle>.

NOTE: Whereas all reference material involved at least three different sources (in some cases many more than three), only the latest and last source has been included for the practicality of this list.

Index